WOMAN WITH A THOUSAND HATS

A Memoir by Denise Kawaii
Forward by Sarah Lyons Fleming
Edited by Ava Roberts
Art by Maggie Love

A KawaiiTimes Publication
Longview, Washington

ISBN-10: 197785530X
ISBN-13: 978-1977855305

Editing done by Ava Roberts. Contact the editor at www.avaedits.com
Art completed by Maggie Love. Contact the artist at www.starkgravingmad.com

KawaiiTimes Publishing
kawaiitimes.com

For all the crazy people who support my cockamamie shenanigans.

ACKNOWLEDGEMENTS

With gratitude and dedication to Michael J. Fox and Nick Flynn* for publishing their memoirs and making them available for me to read. Without their willingness to write and share their own compelling memoirs, this whole book would probably just be a rant about what assholes my dad and ex-boyfriends all were.

Additional thanks to the Longview Public Library** for lending the aforementioned memoirs to me. It doesn't matter what happens, you're always cheaper than Amazon. Don't ever change.

To be clear, this memoir is still going to be a rant about what assholes my dad and exes have been, but there's a sprinkling of wisdom and self-exposure in here that may not have happened if Fox & Flynn hadn't written meaningful stories about themselves first.

*I don't know either Mr. Fox or Mr. Flynn personally. If either of them is reading this right now, please don't sue me for attaching your names to this acknowledgement.

**Use your library card. Those books need you.

ABOUT THIS BOOK

The Woman With a Thousand Hats started at the request of family and friends who seemed to think that my life story was something of note and interest. Although I tend to be self-deprecating about most things, even I have to admit that I'm odd and fascinating. I can always be found working on farfetched projects that aren't on the average person's radar. My life hasn't always been happy, but it has always been full of people and events that propel me from one project to the next in rapid succession.

When I started writing this memoir, it started mostly as a rundown through my professional resume. Although it's becoming less common for anyone to hold the same job for forty years, my resume has a certain whimsical absurdity to it that is unmatched by most job applicants. As I write this, I am in my mid-thirties, and am currently working on my twenty-fifth and twenty-sixth career paths as an author and small-scale farmer. To many hiring managers, my resume screams "Job Hopper." Seeing such a wide range of work may mark me as unreliable and unfocused. If you and I were sitting across from one another in an interview however, I would be quick to point out that I have almost always had multiple jobs running concurrently. I am an incurable worker, and can't help but take on new projects and responsibilities far beyond whatever official job title I've been given. If you need an Office Manager who can also run a soft-serve machine, create advertising copy, negotiate insurance forms, and run personal errands on her lunch break – I'm your woman.

As I have talked more to my readers, peers, and family, I have learned that the interest in me goes beyond my talent for assembling a custom quilt and trimming horse hooves on the same day. While trying to answer the question, "What is a memoir anyway?" I began reading Michael J. Fox's memoir, *Lucky Man*. About halfway through his story of his rise to fame, it struck me that the most interesting thing about Fox wasn't his innate ability to put himself in situations that led to success. It is that he is a real person who has taken the time to self-reflect on his history, share his faults, and is both surprised and thankful for his success despite them.

The remarkable thing about the title I selected before even writing this beast of a book, is that I didn't have to change it after I had my "aha" moment. Even when I'm not working a "real job," I'm still *The Woman With a Thousand Hats*. I've lived under the poverty line, enjoyed middle class, and celebrated my time as upper middle class (its brevity made it all the more worth celebrating). Time and again I battle between my passion of entrepreneurship and my desire to be the perfect stay at home mom. Sometimes I'm a fierce supporter with amazing coping skills, and other times I'm barely holding it together. Despite everything I've survived thus far, or perhaps because of it, I have a tenacity for perseverance that I rely on to get me through the low times.

I hope that you enjoy reading about my trip through time as it unfolds on these pages. Although there are moments in life for which there is no substitute for therapy, often I write my way through problems. Today, I sit at my desk in my father-in-law's basement, writing on a computer salvaged from the business my husband, Keith, and I had to close a year ago before having to sell our house and move back into Keith's childhood home. The last three years have brought incredible loss, and in a time when we thought we'd be conquering the world, we are starting over from scratch like wayward teenagers.

Through it all, I've discovered a passion for writing that has not only persevered many trials, but has been deepened by them.

FOREWORD

I first met Denise when she messaged me on Facebook, about a year after my first book, Until the End of the World, was released and our conversation quickly moved to email. We spoke mainly about writing and home-canning before we got into the general state of our lives, and then, as happens, we delved into personal matters both past and present. Suddenly, we were friends. Because either you have to become friends with the person to whom you tell your life story, or you have to kill them, and I only murder people in books.

Maybe it's weird to offer up your life story over email—or not so weird these days—but she made it easy. As you'll read once I'm done bending your ear, Denise has lived an eclectic life and, well, worn many hats. I think this has given her not only an attitude of acceptance, but also a sense of humor when it comes to dealing with the crazy. And, since I'm slightly crazy and love humor, I plan to keep her around for a good long time.

Over the past three years, I've been one of the people who admonish her to *sit the hell down already*. If you're lazy, like me, you'll wonder where she gets the energy. If you're not lazy, then you still might want to tell her to sit down. She probably won't listen, so you'll just have to surrender and *ooh* and *ah* over her many projects the way I do. In some ways—the best ways—Denise remains that three-year-old who decided she was getting a horse, researched the hell out of it, and then eventually did it. (Yep, true story. Read the book.)

Denise recounts some later events for which I was around—in the email sense of *around*—and I'm here to tell you she handled this recent curve ball with much more grace and far less liquor than I would have. And with a sense of humor—about finances, about relationships, and, most importantly, about poop. Yes, *poop*. (Okay, now you know you want to read this book!)

I already appreciated the lens through which Denise views the world, but, as I read, I grew to further appreciate the qualities I know she possesses: dedication, caring, resourcefulness. I also felt a connection with the qualities that are not so obvious on the surface; things to which we can all relate: uncertainty, sadness, and events we sort-of-wish we had done differently but would never change, as they've made us into the people we are today.

I think that's what I love most about memoir—it's a bridge that connects us to one another. It reminds us that no matter what we think or feel, there is someone out there who can say, "Me, too!" And, if we can't say that, we can marvel at others' life experiences and wonder how we would have handled them. Try on the author's hats, so to speak. At the very least, we gain empathy and maybe learn a little something, and there's never anything bad about that.

So, go forth! Turn that page and dive in. Denise is straightforward, authentic, and always ready to laugh. Those are three things I appreciate in a human and a memoir. I think you will, too.

Sarah Lyons Fleming

Sarah Lyons Fleming is the author of several popular works of zombie apocalypse fiction, including the Until the End of the World series and the City series. Her readers are universal in their clamor for more zombies, survivors and headshots.

WORRIER

I was nine years old when Dad shoved my younger brother and me into the twin fold down benches behind the bucket seats of his little red pickup. He drove quickly out of Hillsboro, Oregon, the sleepy suburb we called home. A half hour later we sped down Highway 217 to the west side of Portland. Any questions Calvin and I had of what was going on were ignored. As we were trained to do, we fell silent and looked out the back window at the road disappearing behind us. It wasn't until we got to Grandma's house that Dad found the vocabulary and patience to speak to us.

Your mom had an accident. I'm going to get her at the hospital. Stay with Grandma. His words were level but his voice was tinged with an urgent edge. Before we had time to say goodbye he was backing out of the driveway.

I didn't know it then, but that night was when my life as a kid went from average middle-class American dream to... not. Looking back on my childhood now, I can still see the way it was supposed to go. We were a happy, Christian family. I was going to grow up in the church like everyone else I knew. I'd continue to excel through home-school. I'd go to college, and eventually be rich by way of my talents. I'd be a happy person throughout. Sure, there would be some bumps in the road, but life would be wonderful.

That's not what happened.

Instead of sleeping in my own bed that night, I lay on the pull-out couch with my brother. We stared at the ceiling of my grandma's living room as we eavesdropped her phone call to someone else in the family. My mom, who had gone on a "Girl's Weekend" getaway, stopped somewhere in Washington state and drank too much. Wrapped up in her excitement for the time away from her responsibilities, possibly worried that her professional therapist friend would ferret out how crazy she felt, she drank until the excitement and anxiety became a dull blur. She got behind the wheel when she shouldn't have. It was a stormy fall day and as she rounded a turn on the narrow road, she hit a patch of wet leaves. To one side of the skidding vehicle was a stony cliff that shot up into the air hundreds of feet. To the other side, a similarly rock-strewn precipice that careened toward a river. The car swerved into the cliff, ricocheting off the cliff face and hurtling toward the swift water on the other side. Somehow, be it fate, or God, or dumb luck, Mom's car hit the lone telephone pole that stood on the side of the road. The impact with the telephone pole didn't do the car any favors, but it saved Mom from falling down the rocks into the river.

The car, a mid-'80s Nova with grey paint and a faded interior, collapsed on itself like an accordion. My mom, a straight-laced woman with average homemaker interests, had a sewing project in the trunk that she was taking to work on over the weekend. The sewing machine hit its indestructible carrying case with such force that the case buckled.

Mom, a lady whose most daring adventure was marrying my dad and moving across the State of Oregon at eighteen; whose most scandalous secret was that she took a nap with the kids in her home daycare midday; whose greatest achievement was singing in a Christian band that made it onto the radio when she was a kid; was so intoxicated that she didn't react to the impending crash. Her muscles didn't tense, her body didn't brace for impact, and since she was loose as a ragdoll hitting the dash, she walked away from the wreckage relatively unharmed. She went to the hospital not for broken bones or internal bleeding, but because her blood alcohol level was through the roof.

That's when everything in our lives changed. Sure, Mom and Dad tried to keep things "normal" for a couple more years, but the problems in their marriage that they'd kept secret were becoming more difficult to sweep under the rug. Mom was a born and bred conservative Christian, and at the time, she didn't think divorce was an option. Her parents were missionaries, her brother gave the occasional sermon, both she and her sister were active in their churches. As a family, we were at church at least three days a week for choir practices, Awanas (Awanas is like Boy Scouts except you get badges for memorizing the Bible instead of learning how to survive the wilderness), volunteering, youth group, Bible study, and home school gatherings. I know that Mom and Dad did whatever they could to hold that white picket fence image together, but in the end, the revelation of Mom's diagnosis of bipolar disorder and closet drinking problem began to uncover too many truths to ignore.

Somewhere around that time, Dad stopped going to church with us. Actually, we saw less of him altogether as he scrambled up the corporate ladder. Rumors of Mom's battle with the bottle spread through our church until kids who I'd known since I was a toddler stopped wanting to sit next to me in Sunday School. Those rumors were confirmed when she started drinking on the way to, and during, church. I remember one particularly horrific Sunday when she was found passed out in the ladies' room.

When my parents decided to divorce, the few friends I thought I still had in the church stopped inviting me to birthday parties and sleepovers. Divorce was the one unforgivable sin, according to the Baptist church we attended in the early 1990s, and it seemed best for them to not associate with the offspring of sinners.

Calvin and I had to drop out of the home school program because Mom couldn't handle the strain of teaching us anymore. I didn't fit in at the public elementary school any more than I had with the church-goers though. In fifth grade, I was reading at a college level. Trivial things that my mom had let slide became points of contention in public school. For one thing, my capital Ws were rounded at the bottom. A resulting verbal assault by my fifth grade teacher, Mr. Hollembeak, while I stood at the blackboard is still something I remember with great annoyance. He was astounded that I didn't point the base of my Ws like every other student, and I flat out refused to rewrite the sentence without the curves. Mr. Hollembeak, if you're reading this, I want you to know that I still round my handwritten capital Ws just to spite you.

Before the night of my mom's accident, my biggest worry was trying to convince my parents that I needed my own room. My brother found great satisfaction in being in my personal bubble day and night. He both talked in his sleep and fell out of bed regularly. We'd shared a room his entire life, but even a nine-year-old knows that it's a little weird for a boy and a girl to live in such tight quarters.

After discovering that my mom – my regular, boring mom – was someone who could drink her way into the side of a mountain, I discovered that I had a whole lot more to worry about.

And I did.

We're still living in the little two-bedroom house on Washington Court and I hadn't yet convinced my parents that I needed my own room. It must be the weekend, because I don't have any of the other kids hanging around. Mom babysits a gaggle of children all aged similarly to my brother and I so during the week we normally have other playmates to distract us from each other. Today though, warm and sunny and full of the technicolor of summer, it's just Calvin and me. He wants to play a game with me. I want to be left alone. Mom tells me that we're going play together whether we like it or not and sends us into our sprawling back yard to entertain ourselves. (Fast forward twenty years, and as a Mom now I understand that an adult's alone time trumps a kid's alone time, but this was a lesson I hadn't yet learned.)

Play with me. Play with me. The chant is relentless. There's plenty to do. We have a pond in the back yard that sometimes has frogs in it. There's a big shed that looks like an awkwardly sized red barn and our dad has built us a fort between two apple trees that looks like an old west jail. We have a metal playground; swings and monkey bars, and Dad cares about our wellbeing enough that he's cemented the feet in tight so the play structure doesn't tilt up or threaten to topple over like my friend's swings do. *Play with me.* Play with yourself, you stupid little kid.

Mom calls out the tiny window from the kitchen that overlooks the bulk of the yard. *Are you getting along?* Yes, Mom. We're in the same yard together. That should be good enough.

I'm seven, Calvin's three or four, and being in the same yard isn't good enough. *Play with me.* Fine. How about Cowboys and Indians? (This was back when we were young enough that it was okay to play Cowboys and Indians.) Calvin has a couple of cap guns. The world hasn't gone crazy yet, so it's okay for us to pretend to shoot each other with them. Back then, the summer of 1988, cops didn't show up and accidentally shoot a nine-year-old brandishing a cap gun. I send Calvin to choose his weapon, glad to have a few moments of privacy under the breezy leaves of the trees while he searches our room for the toys.

He finds the props too soon. I don't get enough time to daydream or read. *Play with me.* Fine. I'm the Sheriff of this here town, and you're a bank robber. I'm the law and I charge you with thievery. Give me your guns. Let's tie you up and take you to jail. A double Dutch jump rope will work just fine. They hang the bad guys in the movies, you know. I'm going to string you up, just like that.

The knots are tied, my brother giddy the whole time. I heave and haul him up into the air from one of the backyard trees. It's probably only a few inches. Mom yells out the window again. *What are you doing?! Get him down from there!*

Calvin's cheeks are flushed, turning a strange color of mottled purple. He's still giggling, at least I think he would have been giggling if he were breathing. I drop the rope and he falls to the ground, gasping and rolling in the long green grass. Calvin survives for at least another thirty years (he's made it to the writing of this book despite having me as a sister). I get in trouble. None of us tell Dad.

Years later, Mom can't even remember that I once hung my brother from a tree. Calvin spends his teenage years helping to care for my horse and chasing my dog through cow pastures without complaint while I go to work. That's the thing about Calvin, he doesn't complain. He's a good kid who just wants a little attention and acknowledgement from his big sister.

HORSE GIRL

When she's feeling nostalgic, my grandmother tells a story about me as a three-year-old. She says I stood up in the back seat of her car (it's unclear if we were moving at the time or not – seatbelts were still sometimes optional back then) and announced, "I'm saving up to buy a horse." For more than three decades she has told this short tale as a testament to my certainty of things I'm doing. I was a wonderfully odd child. I never asked anyone to buy me a horse. In fact, I rarely asked for anything at all. I just decided what I was going to do and then, even as a toddler, I did it.

Before I was fully potty trained, I began saving birthday money, yard sale change, penny-per-dandelion payouts, and any other cash I happened to come across. My scrimping and saving continued through the years. While my brother spent every dollar he ever got on candy and small toys, I continued socking cash away until I had more money in my bank account than my parents did. It really is amazing how much money a kid comes across just for being a kid. This point has been reaffirmed now that I am mother to my own toddler, who saved so much money himself that at the age of four he purchased his own multi-hundred dollar DCC HO scale train engine. But that's another story entirely.

When I was old enough, I started babysitting and pet-sitting for cash and I squirreled that away, too. When I wasn't picking up kid appropriate odd jobs, I spent a lot of time reading about horses and their care. As a result of my research, I decided I wouldn't just save money to buy a horse. I called local stables periodically to keep a beat on how much boarding fees were. I wandered the aisles of tack and feed stores and kept tallies on all the supplies I'd need. I saved enough money to buy a horse. Then I saved some more.

Somewhere in there, I think when I was ten or eleven, my parents gave me a giant box for Christmas. It was the biggest present under the tree and I was completely beside myself trying to figure out what it might be. Deep inside, under layers of packing foam and crumpled paper, was a tiny envelope that held a certificate for ten horseback riding lessons. The instructor for these lessons was named Shaena, a rowdy teenager at our church whose parents hoped teaching me to ride a horse would give her a lesson in personal responsibility. Decades later I still count that as one of the best gifts that I've ever received. The lessons went by in a blur. My parents both tried to sneak in to observe my project, but I was adamant that they drop me off and leave me alone. I wanted my experience to be my own, untainted by a fawning mother or the criticism of a father who didn't think the horse business would stick.

By twelve I felt I was a seasoned horse person. I had been intensely involved in Shaena's horse community, visiting local breeders, assisting in training green horses, showing in both Western and English styles of riding, dabbling in Dressage, and both training for and competing as a cross country endurance racer. Against the odds of my disintegrating childhood, I had pinched pennies until I had a couple of thousand dollars in the bank. That's when I started shopping for my new best four-legged friend.

Before I hit the classified ads, I went to Shaena's father, who owned the horse I had been taking lessons on. I asked if I could buy his horse. Cherokee was a stout, stubborn Appaloosa who was a handful when I first began riding. Over the two years that he was my project horse he had grown into a responsive and willing partner. Shaena's dad told me that when I started riding Cherokee, he would have let him go for a song just to get him out of the stable. But now that he had been fully trained, shown, and polished, he wouldn't sell him for less than $2,500. More money than I had budgeted for a year's worth of care.

This is one of those times in life where I learned that what I want often isn't the same thing as what I need. I was upset following the revelation that Cherokee wouldn't continue to be my barn partner. Despite being so heart-set on him, I wouldn't let anyone else pitch in to make the deal happen. Rather than borrow money from the adults in my life, I began looking at other options. Cherokee wasn't the only nice horse I'd ever met, after all, and it wasn't long before other horses for sale began popping up around me. Because I hadn't begged and borrowed to buy Cherokee and kept picking up odd jobs, I still had money piling up in my savings account. Shaena kept her ear to the ground, I kept taking lessons on Cherokee, and I waited for the next opportunity. A few months later Shaena found a baby Appaloosa who had been orphaned. His dam passed away shortly after his birth and a local trainer took hold of him before he died, bottle feeding him until he was old enough to wean. It was no small task for her and I wish I could remember that trainer's name so that I could tell her how much her efforts still mean to me today.

Understandably, by the time baby Oscar could eat grass hay, the trainer was exhausted and ready to move on. She agreed to sell him to me at eight months old for $700.

My grandma was so proud of twelve-year-old me for sticking with my toddler dream that I would own a horse. She went with us the night we picked Oscar up. We got him loaded in the trailer and got back in the car to follow him to our newly rented stall across town. In the darkness of the back seat, she handed me an envelope full of money. It was close to what I had just paid for the horse. I remember tracing the creases of the folded envelope with my finger in the sporadic light of passing street lamps, in awe that Grandma thought I was doing something amazing.

Months later my parents were finalizing their divorce. As time passed, my world became a roller coaster of sharp upheavals and twisting uncertainties. But in a time when I wasn't sure who loved me, where I'd be living, or which parent (if either) was telling me the truth about our circumstances, I had Oscar to lean on.

I figured out how to train Oscar to ride and pull a cart myself. When we were both older and money was tight, I gave horseback riding lessons on him to kids I knew to raise money for hay and boarding fees. He grew up from a little bay horse without so much as a spot on him into a gorgeous red roan Appaloosa with flecks of brick-colored hair peeking out from under a gray coat. His stall was my safe place when I was afraid. His saddle was my freedom.

It's near Oscar's first birthday. He's too small to ride, but he knows how to carry a saddle and wear a bridle. Every couple of days, I hook a ten-foot rope to each side of the bit, pass it through the stirrups, and give him verbal commands as I walk behind him. It's almost as good as riding, although the view is horrible and if Oscar poops mid-stride, I don't have a lot of room to navigate around the hot piles of shit.

The barn has a long, eighth of a mile driveway and when I get bored of trailing behind Oscar in the arena, I take him for a walk down to the two-lane road. Young and full of energy, Oscar dances around a little and I have to work to keep up. Despite the cautionary tales that adults share, Oscar never spooks on me. Never pulls me too hard. If I ever fall, it's because I'm not watching my own feet. Oscar just stops when my hands lose their grip on the rope. He turns around and comes back to me. Nudges me on the head. *What you doin' down there?*

When I find out that my parents are divorcing, I get angrier than I've ever been. I head to the barn, a safe place to be angry. It's usually empty, aside from the horses. I can yell and scream and no one's around to notice. I decide to give Oscar a bath. He's shedding out his baby coat and looks like a molting parrot. Sheets of brown are falling away, leaving a white blanket below.

Oscar doesn't want a bath. He's antsy. I've been wrapped up in my head the last few days and haven't worked him properly. I've just been cleaning his stall, tossing him feed, and running off to pretend life is normal. He fidgets and dances when I tie him up near the hose, stepping on my foot and bumping me hard with his rump. I lose my temper.

If a horse is being mean – dangerous mean – one way to handle it is to get mean right back. Assert dominance. Be the alpha. But Oscar's never been mean. He's just being an energetic baby. But my foot hurts, my heart is broken, and I'm looking for a fight. I spin around and kick Oscar in the stomach. I kick him again. And again. I don't know how many times.

Oscar knows how to untie himself. He's been doing it for weeks and it drives me crazy. While I kick and flail, probably hurting his stomach with the toe of my boot, he gets busy untying. He slips the knot, pulls himself free and spins around on me. But he doesn't get mean. Doesn't assert dominance. He hangs his head on my shoulder. Gets me to stop kicking. Rests his face against mine.

I cried. I'm sorry today, and know I'll be sorry for decades to come.

CAREGIVER

My first stint as a caregiver began before I was a teenager. We were still living together as a family in the small house in Hillsboro. Dad had invested himself into transforming our one-car attached garage into what he called a family room, but that would end up being the unshared bedroom that I so deeply desired.

The garage bedroom was probably the biggest room in our 900 square-foot house. To enter, you passed through a door in the dining room onto a platform, and then descended a set of stairs into the room proper. Not only did I get my own room, but I also got my own computer with a dial-up modem and access to the green-screen chat rooms that would become my sanctuary when I wasn't at the stable or at school. My room was freedom from the heavy feeling of the rest of the house, and this became a saving grace when my mom suffered from her first big mental breakdown.

Unbeknownst to me, or anyone else for that matter, my mom had suffered debilitating depression for several years. These wallows of depression were punctured by moments of joy and immense productivity. At the height of one of her swings, I came home from school one day to find the entire house repainted. She hadn't needed any help in the project; the mania gave Mom the power of an entire team of day laborers.

Once Mom was diagnosed with bipolar disorder, it was like a switch was flipped. Despite having a diagnosis, her behavior seemed to get more erratic and intense. She stopped getting out of bed on days when she felt depressed, and she surmounted feats of superhuman activity when she didn't. It was like the diagnosis gave her permission to let her crazy out of the bag. *No need to hide your swings, Mom. We've got the symptoms all listed here on paper. Have at 'em!*

My dad, along with most people of that era, didn't give a whole lot of weight to mental illness. Ongoing therapy probably didn't seem like a lot of fun, and nobody likes facing the idea that their dismissal of a person's mental status is part of the problem. So, the crazier Mom got, the less Dad wanted to deal with her.

After Mom's first hospitalization for her increasingly erratic bipolar disorder and continued self-medication, Dad told me that he needed some help around the house. He needed a helper to fill in Mom's shoes while she was gone, and the only person he could think of to help was me. Getting Calvin and myself off to school, keeping the house clean, doing the laundry, fixing our meals, and making sure nobody knew Mom was crazy were now all my responsibility. It was an arrangement that made me feel important and needed in a way I'd never felt before.

When Mom returned from the hospital ready to take on her role as homemaker anew, she discovered a monster that she couldn't get rid of. I didn't trust her to take care of us anymore, partly because of her own unpredictable behavior and partly because of Dad's open dismissal of her position in the family. She tried to assert herself back into the role of mother, but I couldn't let the sense of control I felt go. Instead, I mothered her in ways that she was unable to reciprocate. I became the substitute maternal force in our family whenever Mom was too out of sorts to take care of things, which was often. My unwillingness to relinquish parental control was something that I struggled with immensely on Mom's good days, and is something that has bled through the ties of our relationship throughout my life.

Caretaking for my younger brother and mother gave me a set of skills that has served me well over the years. When my husband became ill in 2015, sending us into a tailspin that caused us to walk away from our previous life entirely, I was prepared to care for him and our toddler in a professional and caring way. Because of my previous experiences with my mother, I could cope with the emotional fallout of Keith's misdiagnosis of Crohn's disease, and I knew all the right questions to ask to get him into more appropriate treatment. By my thirties, I'd been an on-call caretaker for twenty years and there was a strange familiarity to the arrangement that was almost comforting.

But what caretaking from such an early age gave me in terms of skill and confidence, it has likewise stripped away. By becoming my mother's caretaker as a child, I lost the ability to trust others to care for me. I also never learned how to behave the way my peers did. I lost the desire to play, the ability to relax, and the talent of sleep. By becoming an adolescent caretaker, I have acquired great sympathy for others, but have also given up the ability to expect others to care for themselves. After all, I never learned how to care for myself. Instead, while picking up the slack during one of Mom's depressive episodes, I gifted myself coping mechanisms with some pretty dire side effects.

While worrying about what each day would bring as a child, I acquired my first affliction: insomnia. It was an easy problem to keep under wraps once I had my new bedroom. Rather than lay in bed staring at the ceiling while my brother talked about ice cream in his sleep, I could turn on the light to read, or boot up the computer and hope that no one heard the modem dialing the landline. By the time I bought my horse, I was frequently getting less than six hours of sleep a night.

I spent some time in highschool trying to slay the sleepless beast. During a stint when Mom was afraid that I was also bipolar, she sent me for several psychological tests. I was treated for depression and was given medication to help me sleep, but quickly discovered that the meds were only a small band-aid on a very large wound. Beyond my struggle with sleep, teenagerhood also brought on brushes with eating disorders. I was briefly looked at by my counselor for possible anorexia and binge eating. I also had to work hard to overcome dissociative feelings that reduced the world around me to a world that seemed so false that I felt invincible in it.

Now, as a thirty-something person with twenty-something years of caretaking experience, I'm acutely aware of the long-term dangers that taking care of others can bring. By constantly putting someone else's needs before their own, caretakers fall into a litany of physiological and psychological traps. Feeling less important than the patient tops the list, causing a long-term caretaker to feel insignificant. A person only has so much energy, after all. Adding to lopsided self-prioritization, physical exhaustion and mental fatigue make eating right and exercising often seem impossible.

The irony of this backwards phenomenon really hit home for me a few years ago. Mom had fled her mentally abusive second husband. At nearly three hundred pounds she had been diagnosed with type 2 diabetes, and was warned that a heart attack wasn't just possible – it was imminent. After rescuing her from her soon-to-be ex's apartment, Keith and I moved her in with us. I had just left the restaurant franchise where I was a do-it-all office manager, and needed a new project to fill the void. Mom's crisis was the perfect fit; filling my life with a new round of doctor's appointments, Social Security paperwork, a renewed search for a better medical team to take over Mom's mental health care, and the task of teaching her how to live on her own.

In the three months she lived with us I worked to get Mom exercising regularly. I taught her to cook and helped her gain the other life skills she'd need to move into her own apartment one day. But while Mom's waistline reappeared and her ability to take over her own care routine surfaced, I gained weight and stopped paying attention to my own care. Insomnia and night terrors ravaged my nights, and I found myself hiding runs to Taco Bell between healthy home cooked meals.

In my extensive time spent in hospital waiting rooms, doctor's offices, therapy sessions, recovery groups, and crisis intervention groups, a specific question comes up from newcomers to the caretaking game. *How can a <insert professional title here> be trusted to take control of my loved one's care when they obviously can't take care of themselves?*

Here is my answer to the uninitiated. Caretakers dedicate their lives to others, and in doing so they often carry the weight of the world on their shoulders. They are typically overworked, underpaid, and exerted past the point of normal human capacity. While the average person only has to care for themselves, and perhaps the members of their immediate family, caretakers do that in addition to caring for one or more (often many more) people who are in dire situations. I've cared for people with debilitating mental disorders, chemical addictions, food disorders, personality disorders, and physical illness. Spending extended amounts of time with people in crisis inevitably puts you in the crosshairs of someone else's family drama, career tailspin, financial catastrophe, and physical limitations. It's a lot for a person to take on, and compartmentalizing is not only difficult, but depending on the volume of these things that a caretaker deals with daily, may be impractical.

Although I know that my health is important, it is often overshadowed by the immediate need of someone else. It's so easy to put off self-care until tomorrow, or next week, or sometime in a couple of months, or next year when hopefully things will settle out. There are times when making my own healthy choices becomes impossible because I'm simply too tired to try. It doesn't help that finding others who understand can be so difficult for a caretaker, adding a layer of isolation on top of the already volatile mess of other people's drama.

Of course, I didn't know any of this when I was ten years old, refusing to let my mom do my laundry. Or when I was fifteen and understood getting my permit was a pass to be a chauffeur to every hospital admission. It didn't occur to me that I was damaging myself by working full time during high school so I could cover my own bills, pay for my horse, buy my own food, and provide school supplies for myself and my brother. In all those instances, and many more like them, I was just glad to be able to help.

As a pre-teen, the world of adults started to appear completely absurd. Sometimes, the things that the grownups around me were doing were downright stupid. Why work a job that you hate to spend money on things you don't need? Why pretend to like a guy and make him think you're friends and then make fun of him as soon as he leaves? Why compete with your neighbor for better and better stuff, when the things you own are perfectly fine?

Above it all, why pretend everything's okay when it's not?

At a time when my mom was ill, my dad was gone, and I began negotiations with adults by myself for food and care for my horse, I decided to put my frustrations down on paper. I started writing my first book, *My Two Cents: Rules for Adults*, when I was about eleven or twelve. I never finished the manuscript because writing a whole book ended up being a lot more work than I'd initially thought it would be. But I did make it through several chapters of ranting diatribes on how adults should behave from the perspective of a kid who was impacted by their ridiculous choices.

The partially finished work still floats around on a three-and-a-half-inch floppy disk deep in the bowels of a drawer somewhere. I couldn't tell you much of what's on it since it's been years since I've even owned a drive that could read the damn thing. But I do remember the overall sentiment. Adults seem to be oblivious to their own wants and needs, and do ridiculous things to look like they're someone they aren't.

I knew from the beginning that the whole process of chasing after "stuff" to make yourself feel good, important, or successful was a fool's errand. It was clear to me that no one was happy choosing a career based on income instead of passion and talent. As a kid, I knew exactly what I wanted to do when I grew up. I wanted to keep horses and write books, and all I needed to do was to keep doing those two things to be content with life.

Of course, the clarity I had as a kid became clouded as I reached adulthood. Life circumstances would change my perspective on the meaning of success, and an intense anger at my father would eventually create a drive in me to compete with his career in the high-tech industry (which ironically, since we haven't spoken much in twenty years, he doesn't even know is a competition we've been in).

I'd lose my way and get caught in many of the same traps that I'd seen the adults before me flounder in. But for a moment, writing in the middle of the night in a spiral notebook under the dim illumination of a teal desk lamp, I'd begun the career that would thread through my life for decades. I was an author.

COLLEGE DROP-OUT

There is a lot wrong with the United States' cookie cutter college track. Perhaps, not inherently wrong with the dream of higher education itself, but with a person like me fitting into it. As a kid, I wanted to do two things when I grew up; write books and work with horses. Specifically, on the horse front, I wanted to be a jockey in the Kentucky Derby, which I joke at five feet four inches is the only job I'm too tall to pursue (not entirely true, as there isn't a height limit to being a professional jockey – it's the weight limit vs. desired level of sandwich consumption that kills me). For a time, I allowed the pursuit of the college experience to derail me from both ventures.

When I made the transition from the comfort of home school to the industry of public school, there were many jarring shifts in the world around me. First, in elementary school with the curved Ws incident. This was followed shortly after by the discovery that I couldn't visit the bathroom whenever I felt I needed to. Wetting my pants in the middle of class and trying to cover it up as a spilled glass of water when there was no water, on gym day, when the required activity was gymnastics and we were too young for locker rooms and wardrobe changes, was unsettling. But beyond the general "I was a kid who had to learn the hard way how things worked," there was an undercurrent of brainwashing going on. The message was that the only way to pursue a life of worth, was to get a college degree.

In the spirit of Mike Rowe and his championing of the working class, let me say here that I don't think there's anything wrong with higher education. There are many amazing careers out there for incredibly bright people who need to further their book learning to cure diseases, build bridges, and work on projects that I can't conceive of. Should a child be bright enough and filled with enough desire to pursue those things that *need* a paper certificate to prove that they've learned to not kill anyone in their care (unless that's factored in as part of their sanctioned responsibilities), then I wholeheartedly believe that those kids should be pushed to the schools that will best help them in their endeavors.

But (here is where my viewpoint on the schooling industry is less popular) you don't need a degree to work, and it isn't a catch-all solution for a fulfilling and successful life. There is a common misconception today, amid job scarcity and uncertain financial future not only on an individual, but on a national level, that going to college is the only way to get a job that will pay the bills. This idea is simply not true. I don't pretend to speak for everyone, but I can tell you a little bit about my dance with college and assure you that although life hasn't turned out exactly the way I'd planned, it's no fault of my lack of a college degree.

For a while, as a kid who believed that the adults in my life had some sort of interest in my success, I bought into the college dream. I was smart enough; hell, I was taking college reading courses provided by our local community college in sixth grade. By middle school, after having taken my first stab at writing a novel and already having some farm jobs under my belt, I decided that I should abandon those dreams to really make something of myself. After all, that's what all my teachers, school counselors, family counselors, and school-provided college planning staff all said I should do.

I'd like to note here that among the adults crowding my existence as a kid, my parents never pushed me to pursue college. For as long as I can remember, my father has furthered his career by taking college courses between shifts. My mom, too, went back to school to expand her knowledge of accounting in hopes of an office job to support herself. But as a kid and pre-teen, neither of them pushed me to dream of what college I would attend. Unfortunately, because of the problems we were having behind closed doors as a family, I began discounting everything my parents thought of me and my potential, and after my dad exited my life for the first time I cemented a vow that when I grew up, I would be more successful than him. According to my A.P. (Advanced Placement) teachers, the only way to do that was to get on the college track.

Ironically, it was my prolific work ethic that pushed me off the path to higher education. Despite the hurdles at home, I maintained above average grades throughout middle school and into high school. Even after our family split, a mid-day exodus from one parent's home to the other's, rage resulting from adolescent abandonment and a thrust into poverty, I continued taking courses that were beyond those of most of my peers. But faced with the financial reality that I either had to work or give up my horse (he was a pretty heavy line on the monthly budget when we were living with Grandma to avoid homelessness), I started to work after school.

Now, in the '90s there were labor laws. They weren't as strict then as they are today, but there were some pretty big constraints to get around. Kids couldn't work long hours, there was a curfew, and there were no ancillary benefits to be had. A fourteen-year-old simply didn't negotiate vacation or sick pay. It didn't matter though; I was smarter than the system. I quickly began jostling multiple part time jobs, often working seven days a week. By the time I began driving I was holding down up to three jobs at a time. My grades finally faltered my senior year when at seventeen (I was the youngest of my class), I graduated with a C average.

The only discussion with my parents that I remember vividly about my prospects for going to college came on the day of my graduation. After not seeing him for two years, Dad came up from California for the event. When I held my high school diploma, switched the tassel on my cap from right to left, and made it back home to celebrate, Dad sat me down. *Your stepsister is on track for an Ivy League education. With grades like yours, I doubt you'll be headed that way.*

I don't think he knew in that moment, while he was scoffing at the accumulated Bs, Cs, and Ds on my final transcript, that I was also pulling paychecks as a horseback riding instructor, a pet shop clerk, and I'd started working for Nike. The week I graduated from high school, I also put in nearly fifty hours of paid work.

That summer I made the hellish decision to sell my horse. After all, I wouldn't be around to care for him while I was away at college. In true Denise Kawaii fashion, I filled my last summer of adolescence with more hours at work. Once Oscar was rehomed with a distant cousin, I no longer gave riding lessons and turned down offers to train other horses. I quit my long-standing job at the pet store for the first time (I'd be back) and began selling shoes at Nike's employee store full time. And I started a new series of side gigs too because one job – even full time – just wasn't enough.

I was accepted to a technical school that spring, deciding that I wanted to focus on graphic design. I qualified for an almost full-ride, but needed to finance $5,000 for the two-year degree. I couldn't get a parent to co-sign the loan, and ended up enrolling in the local community college instead. Their admissions counselor encouraged me to consider architecture studies (*There's just not a bright future in computer graphics* – HA!), and since I'd gathered enough college credits in high school to cover much of an associate's degree, my first term was saturated with art and blueprints.

By winter break, I was back to cleaning cages in the early morning at the pet store, was still selling shoes at Nike, and had been offered a job as a telephone collections agent. The collections job offered more money than I'd ever made in one place – $26,000 a year plus benefits. I did some quick math and realized that I could either pay tens of thousands of dollars to get a degree in Architecture Design, something that I wasn't enjoying nearly as much as the computer graphic design class I'd taken in high school, (*Come on*, says the guidance counselor, *computer art is just another mechanized fad.*) or, I could make enough money to live on my own.

A salary, rented room, and freedom to pursue other side projects won out. Despite my jump out of the college degree factory, lack of work has never been a problem for me. I attribute this to two traits. First, I'm open to any opportunity. I'll consider any job regardless of how dangerous, unsteady, exhausting, or meticulous it is. This is how I've accumulated tandem jobs on my resume that read: *Sheriff's Deputy* and *Licensed Insurance Agent*, along with *Restaurant Franchise Office Manager* and *Paintball Sales Representative*. Second, I create work for myself when someone else isn't creating it for me. Aside from holding down a litany of regular paycheck jobs, I have always done side sales (I've sold shoes, knives, insurance, paper towels, animals, sporting equipment, livestock equipment, and collectible toys). This second trait, the side project faction of my personality, can be maddening at times because I see opportunities to grow a business everywhere I look. There are simply too many options for me to pursue at once, although you can bet I still try.

Even now, as a thirty-something mother/author/caretaker who is seeking shelter in a family member's home, I don't regret skipping out on college. I'm not someone who looks back on high school as my "glory days," and I certainly don't envy my peers who followed the college track only to discover after tens (often many tens) of thousands of dollars in debt, that their degrees were worthless. For so many, it's only after college that they discover their life's passion or hone a talent that is in demand. For quite a few of us Generation Xers, following our interests in college is a big gamble when it comes time to finding a job that actually trades money for time.

I'm blessed in that I don't have the struggle of feeling like I'm not who I was supposed to be. Although as an entrepreneur I often feel like I've failed (or am currently failing). I don't have an unused degree hanging in my office, taunting me for not reaching some industrialized potential that I was supposed to have reached. I'm not hounded by college debt like some of my closest friends, and I don't feel pigeonholed into anything. My ability to work has very little to do with the magical paper trail of higher education. Instead, I've got on-the-job skills that have kept me employed from everything from bookkeeping to event production and promotion.

The other thing about choosing to not go to college is that it hasn't prevented me from learning. Despite my college advisor's misgivings, I do get to do graphic design on a regular basis. She was right that I didn't need a fancy degree to do it, though. Instead, I've discovered that you can learn how to do just about anything between resources at the library, YouTube, and Google. Study has continued in my life, and I don't think it's truly *despite* avoiding college, it may actually be because of it. Because I never crammed for mid-terms, endured lectures I couldn't walk out of, stressed over finals, and curtailed worry over scholarship and grant approval, I never lost my love of learning. I've been able to continue to pursue education in whatever way was interesting to me at the time, and keeping a pulse on how to find learning resources has served me well as I've moved from industry to industry.

I struggle deeply when faced with family members and friends who are on the push with their kids and college. Occasionally, I step in and gently suggest that perhaps college isn't a necessary thing, particularly when the kid has no idea who they want to be when they grow up. The college experience doesn't have to be a rite of passage into adulthood, and plenty of people find their way without struggling through it. Many of the teens I've known have forced themselves into college to make their parents proud, not as a way to achieve progress in their life's dream.

If asked by any young person about what they should do regarding college, I would say, stop following the educational machine. Don't go just so that you can say you went. Figure out what you want to do in exchange for a lifestyle that you are content with. Don't worry about living on a hill in a big house with fistfuls of money, because that's probably not going to happen right out of the gate. Instead, figure out what drives you, and find a way to learn more about that. Heck, take college courses and get a degree in it if you want! But only invest as much into college as you can reasonably expect to get back out of it.

As for me, I've discovered I don't need to major in English literature to write. I also don't need a Masters in Statistics to know that betting on racehorses probably isn't the best way to return to the horse industry. But losing a few dollars on a long-shot this spring gave me the push I needed to get back to the farm. I'm starting small with farming, hedging my bets and hoping to pull my first big crop in a few months' time. Hell, this past fall I even took a class on permaculture farming from Oregon State University to help me on my way.

My job the summer after high school was to sell Nike products to Nike employees. It wasn't particularly hard, especially since most of my customers were the people who worked to design the stuff in the first place. They knew exactly what they wanted, and I learned quickly to not correct them on their shoe size, even when they were totally wrong.

Occasionally, we'd entertain celebrities and their guests for an afternoon. They'd be given a cart and a spending limit. Typically, the spending limit was more than what I paid for a month's rent. Who needs to be able to buy fifty pairs of shoes? I could tell you, but I'm pretty sure I'm bound by some sort of confidentiality clause.

When the celebrities were in, managers would take them from department to department, schmoozing, elbow rubbing, and generally acting like they were more important than the closed-loop retail store manager that they were.

One day, a celebrity came in. I could let my worries over Nike's corporate policies go and tell you who it was, because I *really* want you to know. But, let's be honest, this book is going to sell so many copies that eventually those Nike execs will get wind of this story and I don't want my first rise to the best seller's list to be tainted with a lawsuit. So, let's just call this dashingly handsome male celebrity HCJ. He has a long name, and if you don't say the whole thing, no one will know who you're talking about, so I've got to use three initials for this story.

So, HCJ comes in and my manager is his handler for the few hours he's there. He was playing a show later that night, so HCJ was keeping a much tighter schedule than we were. He found a shirt that he liked, but he needed a medium and all that was on the floor were smalls and extra larges. That's the problem with the employee store. All the employees throughout the corporation know what's going in there, and they often buy up the really good stuff as soon as it hits.

My manager, a tall bald guy who thought himself to be some sort of sports maven, commanded me to go in the back and find this particular blue shirt in a medium. I told him I thought the size was sold out. I'd checked for someone else earlier in the day, but I'd be happy to look anyway.

Sure enough, there were no mediums. At least, not in blue. I pulled a gray and green shirt in the requested size and took them out onto the sales floor. I started to approach HCJ, and my manager stopped me. *Are you color blind or something? I told you, medium blue.*

I explained again that the blues were sold out in that size. There simply weren't any back there. He sent me back again. I checked the other shirt boxes. Sure, maybe something was misplaced. Actually, no. It never would be. Those warehouse guys ran a tight ship – don't let the guy wrapped in cellophane, hopping around on duct-taped legs fool you. They wouldn't allow you to mispick, and if you brought something back and shoved it in a random box, they'd find you and cut your shoelaces. Not really, but they would wave a box knife at you and make threateningly grumpy faces.

Back on the floor, my manager was chatting up a mousy blonde in the celebrity entourage. I approached HCJ directly and told him that I was sorry, the blue shirt was out in medium. I explained to him that I had it in some other colors if he'd be interested. My manager caught me talking to this mellow, smiling celebrity. Apparently, it was akin to the peasant speaking to the king. I'd stepped way out of the shoe empire hierarchy.

You better have found him that shirt. I explained the situation to both my manager and the celebrity again. I can't bring them something that doesn't exist. *Get your ass back there and find it. I can't believe they made me hire someone so dumb that they can't find a simple shirt. HCJ, sir, I'm sorry for the inconvenience. Let me find someone who knows how to read a label so we can get this sorted out. Denise can go back to the shoe pit where she belongs.*

HCJ's eyes flicked between the two of us. His eyebrows furrowed and his crooked smile turned upside-down. *Hasn't she been back there a couple of times to look already?*

My manager started to berate me some more. He was sure that HCJ never had to deal with this kind of crap with his crew. To the manager, he seemed like the kind of man who knew how to hire people that could get things done.

I think she's done fine. She looked for it, it's sold out. It's not a big deal, states HCJ.

My manager's entire head went red. He said something else – something degrading. I don't remember what. But suddenly he was yelling and pointing his finger in my chest while I shrank beneath his bluster.

Fuck off. My manager and I booth look at HCJ. *Get out of here. I don't want you to be my personal shopper any more. I want to shop with the girl.*

HCJ gestured for me to join him as he moved through the golf section. I moved gingerly toward his cart and pushed it meekly behind him. I glanced over my shoulder at my manager. His glowing scarlet head had swelled. His puffed chest held a breath that contained a yell he couldn't let go of. The celebrity had spoken, and HCJ became one of my favorite people on the planet.

WAIST MANAGER

Growing up, every woman I knew was trying to lose ten pounds. My mom had been on a variety of diets, even sharing her Slim Fast with me on mornings when I was running late for school and didn't have time for breakfast. Grandma ate a strict diet overflowing with iceberg lettuce to overcome her desire for licorice. Aunts, cousins, and friends were all on a quest for the perfect body.

When I was twelve, I had an uncomfortable conversation with one of my uncles wherein he described his disgust with any woman who weighed more than a hundred and twenty-five pounds. I remember telling him that I was near that weight, and his response was that I shouldn't spread that information around. He wouldn't dare be seen with a woman that size, and he didn't see how I'd ever land a boyfriend if I let myself get any bigger.

Mom also periodically chimed in, indirectly and probably unintentionally, about the importance of weight on a relationship. I don't know how old I was the first time she let slip that her relationship with my father became strained the day she surpassed a hundred and thirty-five pounds, but it has come up frequently since then as she continues to process how important physical appearance is in her own life.

The message that I received from these interactions was clear. Fat people are sad and lonely, so don't get fat. Oh, and "fat" meant you were a size eight, within a weight range a doctor might classify as normal, and any effect height might lend to this fatness equation isn't taken into any kind of consideration.

At seventeen, I vowed to never reach one hundred fifty pounds. By then, Mom was in a deep depression and growing rounder every time I saw her. The combination of poverty, mental illness, and side effects of her medications were taking hold right around her waistline. I couldn't understand how anyone could let themselves go like that when there were so many diet options out there.

Imagine my surprise when, after trading my cowboy boots for an office chair, my once wiry body became a little less svelte. My hips rounded, my lower abdomen expanded, and seemingly overnight there were handles to be loved. I was dating a very nice guy at the time my waist began its rebellion, and to his credit my weight wasn't a factor for him. Mike had beautifully thin sisters, but he never compared me to either of them. My issue with weight was my own, although I tried to get him to see what a disgusting slob I'd become as my scale started inching its way past the one-fifty line.

It took me a long time, a decade or more, to realize that what had happened to me was a natural shift in weight. As a teen, I was constantly in motion. Not only was I still pretending to grow (I hadn't changed height since that conversation with my uncle as a twelve-year-old), but I was out in the fields working my horse almost daily. I shoveled shit, moved bales of hay that weighed as much as I did, and chased children around the barn.

Once I decided to get a "real" job, the perpetual motion stopped. I sat at a desk at work for eight or ten hours a day. Then, exhausted, I came home and sat in front of the TV or my computer to unwind. Days off became rituals of doing as little as possible. The funny thing was, my body didn't know what had changed, so I was still hungry as if I'd just loaded a ton of hay into the hayloft. It didn't take long for me to find myself standing in front of a mirror, appalled at the size sixteen fatso staring back at me.

I became a participant in the lie that because I was overweight, I didn't have value. I began exercising compulsively, dieting sporadically, and beating myself up daily over a scale that refused to head in the direction I wanted it to. I did have a couple brief successes in getting my pant size down into the single digits, but each of those successes were a symptom of addictive gym attendance and eating so little as to concern my friends. Most notably, I wrangled myself below the one-fifty line during the brief time I lived in Seattle where my main caloric intake was beer gifted to me at the sports bar, and during my stay in Honolulu where I was too broke to go anywhere other than the on-base gym. During these times, I walked nearly everywhere because I either couldn't afford to drive or couldn't get the engine to turn over.

It wouldn't be until many years later that I would be diagnosed with polycystic ovary syndrome (PCOS). Not only was a shift from the barn to a desk to blame, but beyond puberty my body has been in a constant war with itself. Untreated, PCOS and its inherent hormonal imbalance causes a litany of health problems. Weight gain, excessive body hair, irregular menses, diabetes, heart disease, fertility issues, and depression.

It was no wonder that as a young woman capable of growing a goatee, incapable of keeping my weight in a normal range, battling cramps severe enough for a Vicodin prescription with unlimited refills and menstrual bleeding that was single handedly keeping Kotex factory workers clocking overtime, that I wasn't feeling great about myself. I didn't know what was happening then, and now decades later still only pretend to understand the fight I'm up against. All I knew was that I didn't look like any of the tiny, toned women that my father was chasing. Even if I ate like a rabbit, or nothing at all, I couldn't get myself to look like the women my family revered.

I couldn't see that I was generous. I dismissed comments that I was engaging, entertaining, and hard working. Mike thought I was great no matter my size, and rather than embrace his way of thinking, I dismissed him as someone who just didn't get how important being thin was. I couldn't allow myself to be happy or content if I was overweight, and all I could see in the mirror was fat.

My battle with my bulge continued well into my late twenties when I finally began to wrap my head around the idea that what I was doing to myself was crazy. I opened my eyes to the women in my family who were still riding the diet cycle. They all had the same body shape. Pouched belly, rounded hips, wide butt. They all struggled with other symptoms I had, too. The PCOS diagnosis came in my early twenties, but I didn't really surrender to it until years later when I began to understand that there was more of me to value than what would fit inside a girdle.

Now, looking back on all the pieces that fit together into my body image as a young person, I wish that I'd ignored all that focus on weight. It would have come in handy if I'd brought it up with my doctor with more urgency, instead of avoiding the doctor altogether. An earlier diagnosis of PCOS may not have made controlling my body any easier, but perhaps it would have helped me to understand my own struggle. Regardless of the PCOS though, I wish I'd empowered myself to love any of my other traits growing up. I don't regret much from my life as a young person, but I wish I'd had a different focus on what it was that made me, me.

Outside of the bathroom where I obsessed over the scale, I met the world with defiance and a desire to make something of myself. I've always been overflowing with help and advice when friends or family are in need, and despite being bogged down with self-imposed responsibility that makes attending birthday parties and family dinners often impossible, I've always been the person you can call at two in the morning when you're in a bind (even if it's because you did something stupid). I'm caring, organized, enthusiastic, and I live a life punctuated with impossible feats.

Recently I was asked, "If you could go back in time and tell ten-year-old you anything, what would you say?" My first thought with this kind of question was that I wouldn't go back at all. Despite my struggles, I wouldn't change anything because it has molded me into the person I am today. But as I've contemplated it during the writing of this book, I've come up with a different answer.

If confronted with myself as a ten-year-old, I would tell her that she's okay as she is. I don't have a time machine, and I'm terrible at reading instructions, so I'd probably screw it up and get lost in the prehistoric era if I did. Since I can't tell younger me this bit of wisdom, I'm going to tell you.

It's okay to not fit in with what other people think you should be. It doesn't matter what you look like. It really doesn't. People are going to love you and follow you down whatever path you take regardless of how you look on the outside. You're strong, smart, and you're going places that these people can't even imagine. I'm here to tell you that weirdness has value and you don't need to pay attention to anyone who says otherwise.

It's seventh grade, and I'm standing beside my locker waiting for the bell to ring. I've started making it a point to not be in class early. The other kids have commented that it seems I like learning too much. I'm having a hard enough time fitting in as it is so there's no point in being dubbed the teacher's pet.

We don't have uniforms, thank God. There's been talk about them for years, but the administration can't get the parents on board. Hillsboro hasn't become a silicon forest yet, so most of my classmates are children of blue collar homes. The FFA has a presence here, and at the high school nearby they have a greenhouse and teach students to raise dairy cows. These are not uniform people.

I lean against the locker, talking to no one. Angelina is my best friend, but she's not here today. She's getting her braces adjusted or something. So, it's just me, looking as cool as possible in my oversized long-sleeved polo shirt, baggy jeans, and unlaced hi-tops.

After what feels like an hour, the bell finally rings. I step eagerly in the direction of my classroom now that the rest of the tide of students do the same. Jeff stops me, grabbing my arm. *Hey – just thought someone should tell you that you've got a moustache.*

I look around to see if anyone heard him. They did, and they stare at me, everyone wearing uncomfortable smiles. No one seems to know if they should point and laugh, or stand and defend me, so they don't do anything. I point back at the four hairs he's cultivating on his upper lip. *You're just jealous because a girl can grow a nicer one than you.*

Everyone laughs, then disappears. Jeff and I stand in the hallway alone. He stares at me, fists clenched. I drop my backpack and ball up my own fists. If he hits me, I'm going to hit him back. I won't know that the hair growth is because of a hormonal imbalance for another decade. All I know is that in middle school, being known as the girl who fights back is better than being known as the girl with a moustache.

DEBT SAVANT

Okay, so maybe "savant" is a little bit of an overstatement, but bear with me. As a child, pre-parental divorce, my parents were members of the 1980s *Charge It!* club. Our family was in a fight for position in the middle class and it was a battle that resulted in a lot more effort and excess than was probably necessary. When Dad wasn't taking night classes, he was working second jobs and selling cars for commission. Mom ran an in-home daycare, sold Mary Kay, and worked several craft fairs a year for extra spending money, and each summer we had a giant garage sale where we sold our worldly possessions at a discount to make room for more stuff.

Work ethic. I can't stress enough how much work ethic my parents and grandparents instilled in me with their dovetailed lines of work. But money management was an area where we were all figuring our shit out together. I somehow understood that to reach the goal of owning a horse, I couldn't spend all my money. Or any of my money. If I got a dollar, it didn't burn a hole in my pocket like other kids. I skipped the candy and toy aisles and took every cent I could to the bank.

My mom still marvels from time to time at my ability to save money and eliminate debt. *I don't know where you learned about budgeting. It certainly wasn't from me.*

This innate knack for figuring out how to make ends meet became useful when I found myself living alone in Portland for the first time. Months before graduation, Mom had met a truck driver named Doug and moved into a small rundown farmhouse with him an hour away. As Mom was setting up house with Doug, my Grandma went off on her own romantic adventure. Through with her self-mandated two-year grieving process following my grandfather's death, Grandma met a man through mutual friends and was experiencing a whirlwind romance on the East coast. We'd been living in Portland with my grandma since my mom gained custody of us. My options were to move to a small farm town midway through my senior year, or live with no supervision while Grandma married and relocated. I opted to stay in Grandma's empty house in the city while I attempted to not flunk out of my last few weeks of high school.

At seventeen, I was left to my own devices in the middle of a sprawling city. What could go wrong? Luckily for Grandma and Mom, I was working so many hours that not much happened. Ferris Bueller didn't get a day off. I did, in a moment of poor decision making, attempt to have a friend who was learning massage practice her sensual craft in an empty bedroom. I didn't think anything of it afterward and left the unlit candles, an uncovered mattress, and a mass of dirty towels strung hither and thither while I went to school one day. Grandma's realtor called her with great concern when, while showing the house to prospective buyers, she stumbled upon a scene that I now realize must have looked like squatters had taken over.

Incense-saturated bath towels notwithstanding, my bills kept getting paid, I scrounged up enough food that my school counselor dropped the concern of whether or not I had anorexia, and I kept taking care of business where my employers were concerned. This adult stuff wasn't so bad, after all.

Post-graduation, I attempted to live with Mom and Doug again. I was still a minor, after all. But I'd had a taste of freedom, I was still working in Portland, and the commute was killing me. We all agreed that I'd be okay going to live with my boyfriend's parents, at least until college started (we all know how that ended up). The transition wasn't all that shocking to anyone. I persisted in paying my own bills, contributed to Mom whatever money I felt I could for her and my brother as they continued living in poverty, and made my merry way through a series of increasingly lucrative job opportunities.

All of this culminated in a job offer from a bank. They seemed impressed in my ability to communicate with others, my typing abilities (I tested at ninety-five words per minute with 98 percent accuracy thanks to my unnatural obsession with *Mavis Beacon Teaches Typing*), and my willingness to spend eight hours a day strapped to a headset with a six-foot non-retractable cord.

Now, I'm narcissistic about a lot of things, but I'm not going to pretend that I was the best debt collector. But I was decent at it. Although I'm not pushy or bullish, I'm resourceful. I spent my days having conversations that went a lot like this:

INDEBTED PERSON: *I know I'm past due, and over the limit, but I'm broke and can't pay.*

ME: *Are you sure about that? I'm pretty sure you could come up with the hundred and fifty bucks you need to get this back on track. What day can I note down that you'll send it in?*

IP: *Ma'am, I don't have a hundred and fifty bucks to send you.*

ME: *Are you still living at 1234 Somewhere Place?*

IP: *Yeah.*

ME: *Do you have furniture?*

IP: *What?*

ME: *Are you currently sitting on a couch, in a recliner, or at a kitchen table?*

IP: *What the hell are you talking about?*

ME: *Look, man, if you own stuff, then you can make a hundred fifty bucks. I had a yard sale this past summer and I cleared two hundred dollars selling old clothes and car tires. So, what are you going to do to try to make up the money?*

IP pauses, considering. *I guess I could have the kids help me clean out the garage...*

ME: *Get this debt straightened out and park your car in a clean garage? Sounds like a good deal to me.*

My coworkers were similarly creative, but I wasn't ever comfortable enough to push some of their suggestions onto people. As someone who skips giving blood because needles freak me out, I'm not going to tell someone to sell their plasma. And suggesting someone further destroy their credit just to pay company X is ludicrous to me, so I rarely advised anyone to put their rent payment onto their credit card unless they were already far enough below their limit that they could then turn around and pay rent with the card.

Look, credit card debt is rarely a good thing. It certainly can be a good thing if you have the financial ability, determination, and willpower needed to pay the card off repeatedly. But 98 percent of the population doesn't fall into that category. Most people get a card with the best intentions and then find themselves inexplicably indebted for decades. Save your money, use cash for your purchases, and if you insist on using a credit card, don't charge a payment for anything intangible. If you're going to put yourself into debt, for the love of money, spend it on physical goods that you can turn around and sell when you need the cash to catch up.

Budgeting isn't mentally taxing. You put down on paper what income you have, subtract your ongoing expenses, and look to have something left over to save or invest. That's it. But it is an emotional struggle for most people. If you're having difficulty financially, then I'm sorry to tell you that you've got to take a hard line where your money is concerned. It doesn't matter if you make ten grand a year, or you're clearing ten grand a month. If you're not paying your bills and/or saving for the next big disaster (it's coming, I promise) then...

- Your kids can live without extracurricular sports and activities, or will find a way to pay for their own equipment and signup fees. Not only can they figure it out, but the experience will help them to become better people.
- I promise you can live without cable or satellite TV. You likely aren't using it enough to justify the cost, anyway.
- Also, if you're broke, stop going to the movie theater. Just don't.
- You can get by with a smartphone and Wi-Fi access. You really don't need to be gobbling up data while you're wandering around outside. Clash of Clans will still be there when you go back inside a building with Wi-Fi.
- You don't need to eat out. If you insist on eating out, I can almost guarantee you that splitting meals amongst your family, ordering sides instead of full meals, and substituting

paid drinks for tap water won't impact your ability to enjoy a night out nearly as much as you think it will.

- You don't need a coffee shop pick-me-up before work, a beer after work, and you'll survive without recreational drugs.
- Your family can bond while taking a vacation that doesn't involve a road trip, airfare, or a hotel stay.
- You can start telling friends and extended family "no" where financial obligation or money lending is concerned. Once you get in the habit, you may find yourself in healthier relationships.

Anyway, I was a pretty good debt collector. And I've been able to survive my own monetary crises as they've come. I've never been overly wealthy, but I occasionally have had been fortunate enough to live comfortably, while also having discretionary income budgeted to use helping others.

Fast forwarding to today. As I sit here and write this page, keeping the debt monster under control has afforded me incredible opportunities. Because I invest in myself instead of "things," I've been able to start, succeed, and fail at multiple businesses. It's also provided the opportunity to survive overwhelming medical emergencies and job loss. If I had the chance to go back in time and witness six-year-old me choosing to put my birthday money into the bank instead of into the claw machine at the grocery store, I'd have to tell that version of me that she's doing the right thing.

Now that I'm a parent, I'm trying to find ways to instill frugality in my son. It's a challenging thing to do, especially now when purchases are a mere click away. As a kid, we'd have to get a ride or walk to a store to spend money. Today, with memorized payment methods, linked accounts, and digital transfers, you don't even have to go to the trouble of getting off the toilet before making a purchase. Click. Ship. Done.

My current system for teaching my four-year-old about money is a three-bank arrangement. When he gets money (and kids do for everything from birthdays to random adorableness) we break the cash into thirds. The first third goes into savings to be used at some later date. The second third goes into a giving bank. The giving bank accumulates funds that go toward his purchase of gifts for friends and family, or contributions to causes when he is feeling charitable. The last third goes into a little red bank with "Spend" written on the side.

To my joy and pleasure, my son has inherited his mother's focus on what he really wants, blocking out any distractions. A train enthusiast from birth, this year he amassed enough capital to purchase his own model railroad. HO scale. DCC with realistic sounds and lights. It was an expensive purchase, even for an adult, but it became one that didn't bite his savings too much. There's still money in there, and he has a new savings goal. It's another train, of course.

It's been three weeks since I moved into Mike's family home. He and I shack up in a suite in the basement. His room comes with its own private bathroom and a vintage refrigerator that I've decided to restore. I also repaint his room and remodel the bathroom because now that I'm not commuting, I have an extra hour and a half a day to fill. His parents seem thrilled with the changes. The first of the month is coming, and I bring up rent to his mom again. I've tried talking to both of his parents about rent before, and they always dance around it and change the subject. I've got Sharon cornered now, though. We both have the day off and Mike and his dad are off at a meeting about their family's rental properties.

We don't charge Mike rent. I look at Sharon with a blank stare. I've just turned eighteen and Mike's three years older than me. He also works at Nike, and I know exactly how much money he's making. She assures me that they've never charged him rent. He sometimes buys his own snacks, she says.

That's stupid. I don't know what else to say about it. *I'm paying you rent. I'm using your utilities, and my crap is being stored in your house. $125.*

I tell Sharon I'll pay her each Monday morning. Sometimes my paychecks fall funny, so I might pay the weekly rent a day or two late, but I'll always make it.

No. $125 a month.

I stare again. It's less than 10 percent of my pay. Less than my car payment. It isn't right, but she won't budge. I concede. It's better than paying nothing. I don't want her to think that I'm dating Mike for the money. It's important for me to pay my own way, and if that's all they'll take from me, then I won't look a gift horse in the mouth.

That Christmas, I buy my mom an Audi with leather seats and a power moonroof. It's the nicest car either of us will probably ever drive.

MAKER OF POOR DECISIONS

My exit from collections coincided with a horrible, drawn out break up with Mike, my then fiancé. Our split resulted in me doing the only thing I could figure to do at that point. I made a dramatic escape. I ran not only from the relationship, but from the state of Oregon. As I looked around at the landscape which was not going to result in wedded bliss, Mom offered that I come back to live with her. The farmhouse that she and Doug shared was falling apart, and the property was tied to a well that turned everything orange and sticky. Mom was battling the downside of bipolar disorder and as much as I wanted to save her, at the ripe age of twenty I was ill-equipped to handle either her downward spiral or her progression from aspiring office worker to welfare recipient.

So, I did the only thing that seemed logical. I packed everything I could into my Honda Civic, enlisted Mike's family into a wagon train of movers, and shifted my life to Seattle, Washington. I had no job prospects, no idea of what I would do next, and yet somehow, I convinced my dad to loan me a couple thousand dollars to get settled. As I look back, I have no idea how the loan happened. Dad hadn't been interested in helping me cosign loans for either my car or education prior to the move. But as it was, he loaned me the money and we both kept meticulous track of the debt. He, I'm sure, kept track of due dates and interest accrual, concerned that I'd take the money and run. I did my best to keep ahead of it, hoping that I could prove I had value as a daughter in monthly installments.

My first novel, *Age/Sex/Location: Love is just a click away*, is based loosely on a string of stupid decisions I made during this season of my life. A child of green screen chat rooms, dial-up message boards, and revolving free AOL accounts, I lived most of my life online. I met throngs of people on the internet and for better or worse, met many of those same people in real life. While failing to find work in Seattle, I spent a couple of weeks in Pennsylvania with guys I'd met online days before, then lived part-time in Vancouver, British Columbia with a stoner who probably still lives in his mom's basement (hey, who am I to judge – I'm in my husband's father's basement right now). It's amazing that as I traipsed across North America I wasn't kidnapped, sold into the sex slave industry, or brutally murdered by any of the then-active serial killers roaming the countryside.

I even went on a couple of dates with a guy who fancied himself to be a real-life vampire. Somehow, being offered a medical bag of blood for dinner on our first date didn't preclude me from trying things out one more time.

The break up with Canada (again, as a burgeoning escape artist, I couldn't just break up with the basement dweller, I had to terminate my relationship with the entire Canadian motherland) coincided with me taking a job in downtown Seattle as a telephone customer service representative. The job was in another call center and although I knew I'd hate it, they at least had hydraulic desks that allowed you to stand while you worked, so I felt marginally less like a trapped animal.

Qwest Communications had a couple of things going for them as an employer. First, as a downtown corporation surrounded by paid parking lots, their pay scale was ridiculously wonderful.

Second, their training course was twelve weeks long, which meant I wouldn't have to talk to real customers for a while, an aspect of the job that gave me gut wrenching anxiety.

Enter the big D. You can take that however you want. Sexual innuendo or otherwise, just about all contexts fit. I met a guy online who messaged me from his barracks in Connecticut. We laughed, we sexted, and then nine weeks into my training at Qwest, we decided to get married. The decision saved me from the call center job, got me out of debt with my dad, and moved me to Hawaii, all within the span of a few months. The biggest complaint I get from readers of my first novel, *Age/Sex/Location: Love is just a click away*, is *What kind of woman meets a guy and just decides to get married on a whim?*

Two thumbs straight up. This kind of woman.

I'm tempted to keep referring to David as "The Big D." First, because we were young and dumb and the moniker fits. Second, well, he had a big D. He was a big D. We went through the big D(ivorce) together with neither grace or dignity.

Despite our rushed romance and insane military lifestyle, I took our marriage very seriously. My mom's family is overflowing with missionaries, pastors, contemporary Christian musicians, and devoutly judgmental religious fanatics. I hadn't gotten over being ostracized from the church following my parent's divorce, but I still held a lot of the church's beliefs where submissive housewifery and marital dedication were concerned.

Two weeks after I moved in with him, I knew I'd made a horrible mistake. David wanted to invite his girlfriend to stay with us, and asked me to find a place to be for the couple of weeks she'd been in town. I scoffed that he hadn't even told the girl he had a roommate. *That's a good idea. I'll tell her you're my roommate and you can stay in the guest bedroom. We'll need to find you a bed.*

Now, I was no saint. Prior to our vows, I'd had plenty of experience with males of all fashions and forms. But his holding onto outside relationships past our marital commitment gutted me. Not only that, but David became a giant asshole once we lived together. The flowery love notes and gifts that I was accustomed to during our courtship vanished and were quickly replaced by verbal abuse and indifference.

I called my grandma and told her that I thought I needed to find a way back home. She gave me the advice that any religious woman, married first to an international missionary and then to a radio Bible station manager, would give. *You need to show him a good marriage through your actions. If he's straying, do better in the home. Go to church. He'll come around.*

I was so put down after talking to Grandma that I didn't talk to anyone else about my misery for over a year. The idea that David's inability to be the husband I wanted him to be was my fault for not being sexy, clean, or organized enough made me feel like a new kind of failure. I joined the gym, began obsessively cleaning the house, and learned to not complain about anything. I did put my foot down over that first girlfriend, but to this day I'm not sure how many followed. Like me, David did most of his social interacting online, so there wasn't often a physical presence of outside relations. Grandma counted this as a blessing, but it was no comfort to me.

Our life of marital disaster lasted for two years and two days, David insisting that he wouldn't sign the divorce paperwork until he beat the then two-year average marriage timeline for men in the submarine service. While waiting for the record to pass, I drank myself to oblivion, began experiencing problems with my kidneys because of stress, began dating outside our marriage (I remember a vacationing plastic surgeon, and a couple of other Pearl Harbor transplants fondly), and considered suicide.

The divorce did finally come, and I allowed the Navy to buy me a one-way ticket back to Oregon. As much as I didn't know where life was heading before David, now I was a twenty-three-year-old divorcee to boot. Things weren't looking up, and I knew it was all my fault.

It's 2003. David and I lay in bed in our new home for the first time. We've been married a month, but he had to immediately report to Pearl Harbor and I was still wrapping up life in Washington so we've been apart this entire time. We have the week together and then he's shipping out for his first tour on the submarine.

The new home isn't so new. It was built before the attack on Pearl Harbor and there are breaks in the cinderblock that look like bullet holes. The neighbor says the holes are from the attack. The windows are weird – they're louvered glass and open like the cheap blinds in my Seattle apartment did. They don't close all the way, but that doesn't matter so much. It's hot and humid, and there's no air conditioning.

I roll over and the plastic crunches beneath me. Neither of us have any furniture. It would have cost too much for me to ship mine from Seattle, so I sold it all or gave it away. David's never had furniture since he enlisted in the Navy as a way to leave home. He got us approved for temporary furnishings through the housing department, but everything is obviously used so we've decided not to take the plastic off the mattress. Who knows what's happened on it before.

We hear rain hitting the roof tiles, and we both comment that we're glad it's come. Maybe the rain will cool things down, make the world fresh again. Then a new noise. It sounds like static on an old tube TV, or the ticking of a thousand tiny clocks. The sound drives me crazy, I have to see what it is. David's tired, but he lets me go flick on the light.

Giant ants coat our ceiling. Thousands. Tens of thousands. Hundreds of thousands. Their tiny feet grip the cinderblock and wood beams and tap together in a mass exodus from the rain. Some of them lose their grip on the glossy, overpainted surface and start to fall. It's raining ants, and they are bigger than anything I've ever seen. David flies out of bed and we stand in the doorway and watch the ants writhing through the room. I pound him on the arm and tell him to go grab our pillows.

We take the pillows and a spare blanket into the second bedroom of the house. It's small, but the ants aren't coming this far. They seem content to parade through the master bedroom. David turns out the light and starts to snore. I twitch, unable to get comfortable. I swear I can feel them crawling on me.

I try to sleep, but who would be able to after all that? Well, David can. I tiptoe downstairs away from the creepy crawlies and find something to write with. I need to get my mind off the ants crawling upstairs. That's when the idea for my first novel, *Age/Sex/Location: Love is just a click away*, begins. It isn't a story about bugs. In fact, I don't think there's a single insect mentioned in the whole book.

PUBLIC SERVANT

By the time I made my way back to Oregon, Mom and Doug had gone their separate ways. She was living in a one-room apartment that was barely large enough for her and her dog. I opted to move in with my great-grandparents, a decision that would put an entirely new set of pressures on me. Saying that I was depressed was an understatement. Despite our collective dysfunction, I was still in love with David and wished that we could have found some way to work things out. The advice I'd received from a marriage therapist we'd seen briefly was that I'd either need to accept an open marriage with a revolving set of partners, or find a way to move on.

My great grandmother was an amazing woman. She and her husband, a man who wasn't my biological great grandfather but who had been in her life for the duration of mine, had lived amazing lives and were enjoying the last years of their retirement on a small homestead in Madras, Oregon.

If you've never heard of Madras, that's okay. It's a tiny town on the east side of Mt. Hood, a short drive from Bend's bustling growth. There was opportunity there if you knew where to look, and I somehow ended up being hired as a door tech at the county jail just outside of town.

Being a jail door technician isn't particularly demanding work, and I enjoyed my co-workers immensely. Not long after joining the Jefferson County Sheriff's Department, I was promoted to 911 dispatcher. This may sound like a giant leap in the law enforcement system, but all it really meant was that I rolled my office chair from one end of the secure computer room to the other. I moved from a set of touch screens that activated the locking mechanisms on jail doors to a set of screens that tracked officer movement around the county. I made more money because, as in collections, I had to talk on the phone.

If you have a hankering to get into any level of law enforcement, be it on the ground or as an administrator, I highly recommend going to a podunk town in the middle of nowhere. Most of our inmates at the time were awaiting trial dates for crimes fueled by alcohol or meth. The former generally for peeing on things, and the latter for a wide variety of petty and often ridiculous crimes.

The bulk of the calls that came into the 911 center were for ambulance service, reporting of thefts, or random fires. People were concerned, hell they'd been upset enough to dial 911, but generally once the initial rush of adrenaline faded we'd work through whatever problem they were experiencing and a half hour later I'd be playing FreeCell or Bejeweled on one of the unused corners of the dispatch screens.

The room we tech-based deputies occupied was in the center of the jail, surrounded by one-way glass so we could see into the hallways and cells without being seen ourselves. That was the general idea, anyway. Either the glass was cheaply coated, the glow from our screens was too bright, or it was simply a small town where everyone knew where everyone else worked. Regardless, when I'd walk my dog down to the park, if the jail's work crew happened to be making their rounds cleaning up the trash they'd wave at me and tell me they'd see me later.

It's weird being the outsider – *that girl from Hawaii* – who is recognized by inmates and law-abiding citizens alike. I didn't know any of these yahoos from a turd in the grass. But they all knew me. At least they were friendly.

I was the low woman on the totem pole, so I won the privilege of working the worst shift. Two days, two swings, and a graveyard. If you're someone who has only worked a straight eight or nine hours on weekdays, let me explain that further. Two days sitting down at my desk at 8 a.m., getting home around dinner time. The next two days, I'd roll in sometime in the mid-afternoon and expect to be home by midnight. That makes it hard to keep a sleep schedule, but as someone who has had insomnia since childhood, it was doable. Then the last day, I'd log on in the early evening, work until the sun came up, and the day shift came back to relieve me. My weekends were packed with fits and starts of sleep, trying to recover from graveyard and prepare for the next day shift. The people were great, I loved the job, but that schedule made me lose my mind a bit.

Adding physical exhaustion to my depression wasn't helping my overall well-being. My room in the house wasn't being kept to the rigid standards of cleanliness that my great grandparents demanded. Great Grandma wanted me to help more with cooking, and Great Grandpa insisted that if I didn't make my bed, I was going to give them both heart attacks.

What was the point of getting a divorce? Great Grandma would ask me. *If living alone is so horrible, go back to your husband.*

When Grandma was your age, she was chasing around a nest full of kids, cooking all the meals, doing the laundry, and keeping a proper house. The least you can do is keep your room neat. Great Grandpa would add.

My attempts to explain to them that I was storing all my worldly belongings in a bedroom that was still full of all of their crap (they hadn't bothered to clear the space out for me when I moved in), and that as a modern-day woman I needed to work these stupid shifts so I could get my own house and not live as the spinster in their midst were met with blank stares. The generation gap was vast. From their perspective, I was a woman, my place was the kitchen, and if I wanted to move forward, I best find a good man in town to shack up with or at least convince my ex-husband to come collect me.

I was settling into the dispatcher role despite everything, and was next in line for a regular schedule as soon as a set swing or day shift opened up. These things happened infrequently in a department that small, but one of the senior dispatchers was getting ready to retire and another was preparing to marry her corrections officer sweetheart, so the opportunity would arrive eventually. I saved enough money for first and last month's rent and started looking for a place to call my own.

Most of the time spent in the jail answering 911 calls was comical, and taught me some important life lessons.

Lesson one: If you live in a town with two grocery stores, don't try to run off with a cart full of unpaid stuff. You're unlikely to get that cart of groceries loaded into your car before the cops show up. If you happen to be the Mighty Mouse of load-and-run, making it out of the parking lot with your loot intact, it's likely someone in the store will recognize you and tell the cops where you live. If neither of those two things happen, you are in the extreme minority. Congratulations on your success! Now you have to move, because the next time you need to run to the store for milk, they're going to spot you browsing the dairy aisle over the cameras, and the cops will be there to collect you before you've made it up to Customer Service to pick up your next carton of smokes.

Lesson two: Don't be a frequent flier. Someday, you might be in a season of your life where you get shit-pants drunk and pass out in the crosswalk on Main Street. When that happens, you want people to be concerned for your health. You don't want to be the guy who, when some Good Samaritan calls 911 on your behalf, the response is, "Are you sure he's not breathing? Sorry, we get calls about him pretty frequently and EMT's won't respond unless someone's at least poked him to see if he'll just wake up and move on."

Lesson three: Don't be a shitty neighbor. If you've got a problem with the guy next door, don't shoot him. Build a fence that is right on the property line (*not* six inches over) and move on with your life.

So, I was getting used to the pulse and flow of my tiny five thousand resident town. I gave up being freaked out over work crew at the park and just smiled and waved back when they noticed me. I started looking at rentals around town and had put down a deposit on an adorable one bedroom stucco house on the high desert when the worst happened.

I took a call. A frantic woman on the other end of the line was sobbing at me to send an ambulance. Her son wasn't breathing. We went through the standard steps, followed the instructions on my emergency response checklist. It was an otherwise dead night when she called. I don't remember now if I was on shift alone, or if my backup was just letting me handle it since I wasn't wet behind the ears anymore but things went south. Her son died waiting for the ambulance. My voice over the landline that connected us hadn't been enough to save him.

The rest of the shift was interspersed with the standard nighttime calls. Clogged toilets. A guy pissed off because the neighbor dog was shitting in his yard. Stupid, small town stuff. By the next day, the gravity of the boy dying hit me. I called in sick and spent the day trying to be the housemaid that my great-grandparents wanted me to be. I drank after they went to bed, smoked a pack of cigarettes, and cried when I realized I had to go to work the next day. I couldn't afford to sit at home and process my emotions.

The rest of the week, I avoided answering the emergency line. To the public, there was no difference. As long as someone else was sitting at the other terminal, they'd pick up. I simply stopped trying to beat them to the punch. I took some extra smoke breaks when it was slow. I got a water bottle and decided to hydrate my way into a 30-minute bathroom cycle.

I knew it was only a matter of time before someone caught on, so I spent my next days off putting in applications to jobs over the mountain in Portland. I was quickly hired by an insurance company who needed licensed agents, followed immediately by an offer to work at a banking call center in Beaverton. I'd work the bank phones while studying to get my insurance license and get out from under the scrutinizing gaze of my family. The only way someone would die on the phone at the bank call center was if my telling them the truth about their adjusting interest rate gave them a heart attack.

It worked out for me, but I felt utterly disgusting as a human being for leaving the Jefferson County crew. I wished I could have sucked it up and moved forward with them, but it just wasn't in the cards. I was already teetering on the edge of substance dependence with my incognito drinking schedule and I knew that if the scenery didn't change, I'd soon be spiraling in my downtime as so many who stick with law enforcement do. I let the rental company know they'd have to rent the house to someone else, sad to see my deposit money go, but not upset enough about it to fight for it back. I put in my two weeks' notice at the Sheriff's Office and began driving the two-and-a-half-hour trip back and forth to Portland every time I had a free afternoon to look at apartments.

To this day, I hold corrections staff, law enforcement, and emergency personnel in the highest regard. None of them are paid enough for what they do, regardless of if they're working a major metropolitan center, or if they're in a town where a bad call only comes in a couple times a month. The overwhelming responsibility that those people take on to protect their neighbors, defend the defenseless, and keep the riffraff in line is something that common citizens rarely have the opportunity to grasp. I was glad to be one of them, and am blessed to know that should something horrific happen in my life, they're there waiting for my call.

Charlie21, do you copy?

A call for a stolen car has just come in over the radio. It was called in by a sheriff's deputy out on the high desert, but they're rapidly racing into town.

David7, I copy.

Charlie21, Plate run. Oregon plate. Zebra Victor William 2-2-7

David7, copy.

I'm sitting at the next console. Penny is on the radio. She starts running the plate. It doesn't take long, a half minute or so for the green screen to populate with the information from the DMV.

David7, Vehicle is a 2003 Mitsubishi. Confirm.

Crackling sounds come over the radio. We hear David7's engine rev over the static. *Charlie21, affirmative. Suspect is making a run. In pursuit heading south on US 26. Backup needed.*

I look over at Penny. People don't tend to run on the cops here. She looks back at me, eyes wide. *David7, confirm location?*

Charlie21, we're crossing Poplar. Let PD know. See if they can cut them off.

I get on the radio with the city police officer on duty. He races from where he's parked by the high school toward the end of town. We don't have long to cut the guy off, the main drag is less than a mile long.

David7, vehicle is registered to a Denise Kawaii. Confirm, red Mitsubishi.

I look back at Penny. Her face is inches from her console. She's reporting that there are no warrants tied to the vehicle. Of course there aren't warrants tied to the vehicle. I had to pass an FBI background check to work here.

The radio chatter goes crazy. The city police just missed my car and the deputy as they raced downtown. I scoot around the corner and try to read Penny's screen. My name is there. My vehicle description. Some asshole is taking off with my car, headed toward Bend where they chop up vehicles for profit. I've only owned the car for a few months. It's the only thing of value I own anymore. The thief hits the gas harder when the highway merges back together, tuning into Highway 97, right by the Taco Time where I had lunch earlier today. He swerves and almost loses control, hard to do in the all-wheel drive. They must be going faster than I thought.

They fly through the dry farms of Metolius, on through Culver, and out toward Crooked River Ranch. There's a bridge across a ravine. It's the bridge where most of the attempted suicides take place. Where people sit on the edge and contemplate the drop into oblivion while our deputies close the highway and try to talk them into coming back onto the road. The carjacker races toward it, our officers keeping close. They attempt a pit maneuver, but my car holds the road. There aren't any officers to call from beyond the bridge. It's the middle of the night and the officer and deputy currently in pursuit are the only ones on the clock. I hold my breath as I listen. The driver is wild, hits the edge of the highway and skids in the gravel beyond the pavement. They're right at the edge of the ravine and I imagine my car missing the two-lane bridge. My heart is pounding in my ears. Penny has the radio and I motion that I'm going to have a smoke break. She waves me out.

I fidget as I wait for Misty to open the secure doors, rush through the lobby and out into the cool night air. I take two steps through the lobby exit and stop dead in my tracks. A buzzer goes off and a crackle sounds through the after-hours intercom. Penny tries to say something, but she's laughing so hard that I can't understand a word she says. I shake my head and let go of the door that I'd had in a death grip. I fish out my pack of cigarettes and a lighter, and sit on the curb. I smoke and sit and stare at my car, parked right where I left it. The howling laughter from the intercom buzzing in the otherwise quiet night.

MOVER AND SHAKER

Way back when I was still married to David, living in military housing on Oahu, I got myself a puppy. He was a cute little thing, just a few weeks old. By the time I got my U.S. Navy issued ticket home a few months later, he was a massive beast who I had to put on a diet to get under the seventy-four-pound limit to ride in cargo on the flight back to the mainland. Once we got to Madras, he'd gained another twenty pounds.

Goliath filled much the same role for me that Oscar had as a teenager. He was nearly the same size as a horse, a Boxer/Great Dane mix who looked like he could eat a toddler. He was the best dog in the world though, and despite needing to move around for a while I refused to let anyone take him away from me. I'd even worked primary ownership into my divorce decree, a clause that the court clerk felt was flippant, but that dog was the only thing keeping me from going off the deep end.

Now, I don't know if you've ever tried getting a lease on an apartment when you have a nearly hundred pound, four-legged beast by your side, but it's not an easy feat. I also had a limited rent range that I could afford. My brother was planning on splitting rent, but that didn't count for much because, well, let's just say that if I were more of a bean counter, I'd be bitter that he couldn't pay rent for a few months which resulted in my almost being evicted. (To be fair, he had sold an expensive ring to a couple from Craigslist and they paid him with a stolen money order, putting him behind the ball through no fault of his own other than that he trusted a stranger to not be a dick.)

But I digress.

Hunting for an apartment isn't easy in the first place, but doing it with a giant brown slobber troll in tow doesn't help. I looked at several horrible apartments around the Portland metro and there was a common recurring theme. Dilapidated as the apartments may have been, I didn't want to have the nicest car in the parking lot. I'd just committed to paying $300 a month over four years for the nicest car I'd ever owned, and I didn't want to move in and immediately get car-jacked.

After touring a series of increasingly depressing potential homes, I was about ready to throw in the towel. Maybe a lifetime of utter misery and dying children on the emergency hotlines wouldn't be so bad. I was seriously considering pulling my two-week notice from the Sheriff's Office, sure that they'd happily shred any evidence that I'd wanted to quit and putting me back on the schedule like nothing ever happened.

I decided to look at one last apartment. The place wasn't exactly clean, but it had the air of a maintenance staff that at least tried to cover up the misery with enough paint to be passable if you squinted your eyes. They'd accept my giant dog without too much fuss, and better yet, the car parked next to the spot I'd be assigned was newer, shinier, and more expensive than my mid-range SUV. I was sold.

It wasn't until months after I moved in that my upstairs neighbor (who eventually married me – the weirdo) told me that he was surprised they moved someone in so quickly. Apparently, the complex had recently had a drug raid and it turned out that my apartment had been home to dozens of marijuana plants, which was illegal at the time. No wonder the complex was eager to accept my spotty rental history, giant dog, and job offer letter that looked like it had been Xeroxed in a back alley. They were just happy that someone was dumb enough to rent an apartment that had recently been stormed by the DEA.

My brother moved in, helped me arrange our sparse furniture in such a way that it looked like we weren't a couple of losers, and joined a band. I started hanging out with the guy upstairs, and he put up with me dragging him to my brother's shows around town. I finally got started at Wells Fargo and began my hateful dance around the grey cubicle and six-foot-long corded headset that tethered me to home mortgage accounts.

I started insurance school in the middle of all this transition, and I quickly decided that I was glad I skipped out on college. A notorious skimmer of instructions, I battled through lessons on insurance litigation, Oregon State law, and how to determine whether or not the person buying a policy is planning to murder the intended insured for a payout. Keith, my neighbor turned boyfriend, supported me through it all. When my brother moved out, leaving me to fend for myself with the rental office's past due notice looming, Keith let go of his opulent upstairs apartment and came to live with me in the dungeon downstairs. He found my desire to be my own woman refreshing, dried my tears of frustration when things were harder than I'd planned, and encouraged me to walk away from Wells Fargo the second I had my license in hand.

Once again, I was broke, working insane hours, and trying to force myself to be the pushy salesperson that every lead agent wanted me to be. What I couldn't provide Keith in financial stability though, I made up for with tours of Portland, unexpected visits to dark grungy theaters where my brother's band played, and what I assume was the companionship that he needed as he explored his own cubicle-dwelling career in the tech industry.

I told Keith up front that a life with me might not be easy, but I promised it would be interesting.

Not enough people are afraid of large dogs. This is my conclusion after decades of observation as a dog owner. It seems that the larger your dog is, the more mothers want their toddlers to come up for a pat, and the more frail old men want to lean over them to coo. Goliath was a magnet for anyone with ambulatory problems, be they from a soggy diaper or the weave and bob of muscle degeneration. In general, we treated those who wanted a pet with mild irritation, giving in to their request while Goliath fought to stop the momentum of finding a place to poop while I explained to the children (and their parents) that you should never walk up and grab a strange dog.

In our apartment complex, the kids all wanted a piece of Goliath. Big and brown, he was like a teddy bear come to life. It made getting him to go potty before work a constant adventure. I'd be glancing at the clock on the wall nervously while peering through the blinds at the courtyard beyond my front door, trying to time his walk with kids being called into their apartments for lunch or finding something on the other side of the complex to explore.

One day, we were making the rounds and mid-shit a little girl walked up and started grabbing Goliath's ear. He looked at me with a, *Really? Now?* look and I started in on my spiel about how dogs are dangerous, especially for little girls.

What's his name?

I always answered. There would be a flutter of anxiety afterward, a worry that some person would come back and try to coax my dog into their car, drive away with this friendly beast who loved everyone.

Goliath, Goliath. I love you, Goliath. The girl swung herself over his body, attempting to ride him.

I coaxed her off and started back on my way. Usually, people watch with disappointment when you start walking, and you just point to your dog. *He's gotta go, so I gotta go. See you next time.*

This little girl followed us around the courtyard, up to my door. No parents in sight. No one checking up on the stranger leading their daughter away with a puppy the size of a pony. *Thanks for walking with us. Have a good day.* I unlock the door, head inside, and pull the leash off Goliath. I'm back in the kitchen when I hear the door latch closed again and I look up, expecting to see Calvin or Keith. Instead, the little girl is standing in my living room, hanging on Goliath.

He's just the best dog. He's my best friend. I'm going to visit him every day.

I stutter, motioning toward the door. The girl doesn't move and I have to physically remove her from my apartment and lock her outside. A half hour later she's still out there, talking to Goliath through the door. He's confused, and I'm still wondering where her parents are.

For months, the little girl would show up at random and try to come inside without asking. I don't know her name, and if I asked her where she lived she'd just point vaguely across the courtyard. *Out there.*

When we moved from my apartment into our first house, it was exciting on many levels. First, we were moving up in the world – away from the revolving rent cycle and into a lower middle-class neighborhood. Second, the ceiling in my room had started to leak and the maintenance crew had done a shitty job of fixing it. I looked forward to not having a leaky ceiling, gallons of liquid being retained by a half inch of latex paint. But the biggest relief was that the little girl wasn't outside the day we moved. She didn't follow Goliath into the U-Haul and couldn't shadow us while he tried to pee and I tried to find an adult.

INSOMNIAC

It's two minutes after midnight on a Wednesday morning, just before Christmas in 2016. Today we took our little boy to the museum. There, we met up with my best friend and her two-year-old for a day of joint family fun and adventure. The museum in question is about an hour and a half from home, so we were in the car or chasing astronauts and turning the gears on gantry cranes all day. I'm utterly exhausted. And yet, here I sit, pounding away at my computer.

I don't know where this chapter should go, as I've been an insomniac since childhood. Lack of sleep continues its blight on my existence today, twenty-six years after my first remembered dance with sleeplessness. I'm just going to plop this chapter right here and should the editors decide it belongs elsewhere, I'll let them move it. They are, after all, better rested and likely clearer headed than I.

My first memory of insomnia was around the time my mom first disclosed that we weren't going to be doing home school anymore. I remember lying awake on the top bunk, staring at the ceiling until the sunlight crept in through the window, announcing that our first day of "real" school had begun. Stuck in a room with my little brother provided the night's entertainment. Calvin both talked and was physically active in his sleep, so the night was filled with conversations about unicorn ice cream and punctuated with the sounds of him rolling out of bed, onto the floor, and stumbling his way back under the sheets.

Sleeplessness is something that I kept mostly to myself from the beginning. With it, I could enjoy solo trips to the bathroom (our house only had one) and read uninterrupted in the living room. As I advanced in technical skill and became acutely aware of my parents' sleep schedules, I was also able to use those late and early hours cultivating friendships in chat rooms on the internet. The speaker on our dial up modem was the only hurdle there, but the scream of the modem was averted by a pile of pillows in the early days, and was eventually muted with the help of one of my secret internet companions.

Privacy and freedom notwithstanding, I also learned to not talk about my inability to sleep because I was tired of feeling like there was something wrong with me. As life lost its stability, I was thrust into a world of counselors and therapists, teachers and other concerned adults who seemed intent on "fixing" me. Resourceful as a pre-teen, I read about all the reasons why sleeplessness was bad. Insomnia can cause or exacerbate a laundry list of conditions. From depression to an increased risk of accidents or heart failure, it's generally accepted that not sleeping is not good. So, I decided to keep this part of me out of the psychologist's scrutiny.

Now in my mid-thirties, I've been having trouble sleeping for most of my life. There have been times, particularly around big events like tests and vacations, where the insomnia has gotten to me. I've been a part of several insomniac support groups over the decades, and I feel great empathy for anyone complaining of multiple days with no sleep. Being awake so much can, and does, make daily life feel impossibly out of reach. But, as a multi-decade survivor of this affliction, I can honestly say that I have made the most of it.

One of the worst things about insomnia, and it is the very thing that got me aggravated enough to walk down two flights of stairs to my computer, is the act of lying in bed and waiting for sleep to come. Now, I know that everyone has those nights when they just can't "turn off." (At least, that's what people tell me whenever it comes up.) But for me, and many others, that feeling doesn't just produce a mild irritation that can be complained about over coffee in the morning. For me, the tossing and turning boils quickly into an intense rage. The flames of my anti-sleep fire are fanned by the cooing noise of my sleeping child down the hall and the soft snores of my husband in bed next to me. I love them, but some nights I just want to punch them both in the face.

But alas, dear reader, violence isn't the answer.

Many years ago, I decided that if I couldn't sleep, I was going to get up and do something. The idea is that I'll wear myself out and then try the bedtime ritual all over again. It's one of many practices put into place by insomniacs trying to avoid sleep aid addiction, and as a self-diagnosed addict I'll do just about anything to avoid taking those pills. So, somewhere in my teens, I made the decision to just get up. Getting back out of bed, flipping on a light and doing something mundane like folding the laundry got the nervous energy out of my bones and gave me time to sort the thoughts in my head. I've generally avoided music and television during these bouts of wakefulness because, as I've said before, I enjoy the privacy of the middle of the night. Nothing spoils the blissful feeling of midnight solitude like a cranky family member stumbling in and asking you what the hell you're doing making so much noise.

In my twenties, out of school and thus out of homework to catch up on, I started writing at night. Truth be told, most of my books are written and edited between two and four o'clock in the morning. Even on nights when I'm "sleeping well," I frequently wake up with a start and text myself an idea for review in the morning. Indeed, the advent of the smartphone has been a blessing and a curse for my sleeplessness. On the one hand, I can work in short bursts or commiserate with my list of likewise afflicted friends without getting out of bed. On the other hand, my delight with middle of the night productivity from the comfort of my own bed is only as good as the man lying next to me. The installation of a blue light filter has been a godsend not because it filters the light for me, but because it eliminates the light shining brightly enough to wake my husband.

Here, following the statement that I use electronics in bed, the voice of every sleep professional and advice columnist on the planet rings out in my head. *"Oh, Denise! That's your whole problem. You've got to stop using screens an hour before bed, and banish them from the bedroom."* I've read the studies, too. I've tried removing my phone from my bedside table for extended periods of time, and I promise you, it doesn't make a lick of difference. Nor does the time of day I shower, the type of herbal tea I drink before bed (decaffeinated, of course – I am intensely affected by caffeine), the amount of exercise I get, the structure or timing of my diet, the levels of stress in my daily life, my propensity for illness, or a litany of other outside factors. Very little seems to make any improvement on my sleep. I appreciate your concern for my well-being, and I kindly ask that you place any suggestions you may have for a better night's rest firmly and solidly up your ass.

I've tried all the tips and tricks. I promise. During fits of exhaustion not sated by in-bed screen time, what works for me is what I'm doing right now. I stop fighting the pillow. I plant my feet firmly on the floor, fish my cellphone off the night stand, and use its dim screen to light my way back into the main house. I make myself some tea (tonight it's lavender and honey), wake up my sleepy computer, and weave words together until my mind is quiet and my eyelids are heavy. Despite the aggravation of not sleeping like the rest of the world, this is where the magic happens.

A couple summers ago, I finally got my books into a local bookstore. Jacobsen's Books was on Main Street in Hillsboro, Oregon, and in an effort to not have their storefront glanced over by the thousands of people at the weekly farmer's market out to buy asparagus, they started having local authors come out to sign books. I had the repeated luck of having my book slinging scheduled on two of the hottest days of summer and in the ninety-plus degree heat, a woman asked me when I find the time to write.

Usually at two in the morning. I don't sugar coat my schedule.

I was then assaulted, lovingly, by this motherly figure. How dare I allow my insomnia to go unchecked long enough to write an entire book? She warned me of the health risks, offered several solutions to my malady, and then looked to me with eagerness as she awaited my thanks for her help. I didn't thank her. Instead, I asked her if she'd read any pages of the book she was currently holding in her hand.

Oh, yes. It's so interesting! The short would-be mother figure offered.

Well, to all of you out there demanding a cure for my exhaustion, if it weren't for the insomnia, there wouldn't be any books. Not a single one. The insomnia is as much a part of my writing process as the way I sit lopsided in my chair, the way I squint at the screen when I'm trying to find the right set of words, and the exuberant clatter of my fingers on the keyboard. Chronic though my affliction may be, it allows me the space to wander the world alone without interruption from children or deadlines. I may not be perky in the morning, but most nights I wouldn't trade the midnight ramblings for anything. It's when I'm able to flex my imagination and process complex ideas. If I were asleep and dreaming like the rest of you, there'd be no one awake to write any of this shit down.

Now that the clock has ticked forward to a quarter after one, I've had my first long yawn of the night. The buzzing of my brain is beginning to slow and I can feel my blinking eyes grow heavy. It's time to try the bedtime ritual again, the same way I did four hours ago. Let's hope this time it sticks. If not, maybe I'll get another chapter in before the sun rises.

A new pain has begun. An invisible knife cutting into my neck. For once the pain isn't a result of a tumble or fight. No bruises surface, just a piercing, shooting, aching pain that makes me want to stay still even though staying still hurts just as much.

It takes me weeks of booze and Vicodin before I finally call the doctor. But the doctor I'm calling isn't the one I'm used to – it's my first round of fun with military medical. Nothing is as new, shiny, or clean as I expect it to be. Everything is worn around the edges, the office chairs stained. They've seen worse than me before.

I see the doctor and describe the pain. *Carpal tunnel. Very common. We can do surgery as soon as next week. Eight weeks' recovery time. Limited typing.*

I'm confused. My wrists are fine, it's my neck that hurt. Limited typing? Eight weeks? How successful will this surgery be? I'm writing a novel. All my friends live in chat rooms. A collection of people from across the ocean in a smattering of different time zones. I play games with my best friend in Chicago at three in the morning, the volume turned down on both of our computers while her kids sleep and the neighbors on the other side of my thin walls do the same. I send three thousand text messages a month. My life is online, nothing outside suits me. I live on an island in the middle of the sea, nothing to do but go to the beach and I'm afraid of the water.

Sometimes the surgery helps. Sometimes it doesn't. Hard to say until we do it.

Carpal tunnel syndrome is a result of repetitive motion. The tendons and muscles swell, putting pressure on the nerve. My nerves are sending pain signals up into my neck, because nothing about me can ever be normal. I type ninety words a minute. I send a hundred texts a day. I've spent years being paid to talk on the phone, so now I avoid it at all costs. Send me a text. Send me an e-mail. Write me a letter and send it by carrier pigeon. I can only survive the surgery and recovery time if there's a guarantee things will be better.

About half the people we do surgery on see positive results. Some of those people have to have the surgery again if they don't change their habits. You've got it in both arms. Best to do them both at once.

I shake my head, ignoring the stabbing pain. No surgery if there's no guarantee. I go to the pharmacy and buy wrist braces. Visit a physical therapist and he gives me some exercises.

I cut my writing for a few weeks. I only send a few dozen texts a day. I do the wrist exercises in front of a desk lamp and cast a strange shadow puppet show on the wall. Twice a day. Ten repetitions. *Come back and see us if things don't improve.*

I never bring up the carpal tunnel to the doctor again. I buy new wrist braces whenever holes appear from where the braces rub against the desk. Now, ten years later, I'm writing this book on the heels of another. *Biocide* followed by *Woman With A Thousand Hats*. I need to find my wrist braces. There's a pain in my shoulder – the one on the left. No point in bringing it up, I know what it is and it'll go away the next time writer's block hits.

Woman With A Thousand Hats

PARTNER

From high school onward, I was a serial dater. When in a relationship, I was usually committed, but I didn't bother pretending that a line of suitors wasn't waiting for my current relationship to end. For the longest time, I saw it as funny. *You want to buy me a drink? I'm with someone now. Take a number. I'll call your name when it's your turn.*

In most of my relationships, there were other women. In some of them, I was the other woman. Either way, I came to expect that no matter how good a girlfriend or wife I could be, it would never be enough. Sometimes I knew about it, sometimes I only suspected. But the feeling that monogamy was a fantasy was always there. Infidelity had been there for my mother, and it would be there for me. A relationship flaw inherited through blood and circumstance.

Once a cheater, always a cheater. I believed it for others, and suspected it for myself. It was something ingrained. Learned at birth. Impossible to do without. Every boyfriend I had would eventually admit to having slipped up. A mistake of a night with a girl met at a party. Another relationship started before he bothered to tell me ours had ended. Meeting the perfect guy and having romantic dates near the ferry – under the bridge, out of sight, then being told gently by a friend that my boyfriend was getting married. A husband whose exes warned me he'd stray, my hope they were wrong and discovery that they weren't. Midnight dates on base with someone else as lonely as me, not hot and heavy like horndog teenagers – just deep conversations by the water like forgotten orphans. Finding someone new, or old – from a past life. Reconnecting and thinking this must be it. Meant to be. Then six months of no phone calls. When he finally turns up again and I ask where he's been, his voice is unsteady. *I was working on something.*

Other lives. Other wives. Ladies of the night. Commitment and monogamy a fairy tale told to children because the truth is too scary. Visiting the doctor and asking for tests because even though I'm married, I can't be sure someone else's virus isn't floating through my veins.

I did my best to be a good girlfriend, fiancée, and wife. I cooked and cleaned, discussed child rearing (*if you can stay out of the brig and keep from getting demoted for six months, we'll try*), set up house, and kept my nose clean aside from the Vicodin prescription that still hadn't ended and the half gallon Jack Daniel's bottles that I bought cheap at the Naval Exchange.

After the divorce, I got serious with a guy called Thumbs. He was clean cut, from a good family. Parents still married even though he was in his thirties. He lives with them, of course. All the single men seem to anymore. Stayed in his childhood room, although he'd covered the playroom floor with a king-sized bed and replaced his band posters with a giant TV mounted to the wall. He had a job, a plus, and he talked about wanting to settle down. He'd never cheated on a woman, didn't understand anyone who'd cheat. I don't tell him I've done it myself, hoping that I'd settled that flaw in my relationship system.

Thumbs had a secret, though. A trick that kept him from cheating. Friday through Sunday he spent his time at the strip club. It didn't bother me at first. I tried dancing for a minute in high school when money was tight and opportunities were limited (*sorry, Mom*) and I know how things go down there. He didn't make enough money to be granted special favors, at least I didn't think so. A few dances here and there, no big deal.

As we got more serious, I started staying overnight. We talked about me moving into the family home and playing house while his parents puttered nearby. There was only one problem, though. Thumbs liked to look, liked the dancing, liked to see the moving parts of the female body on display, but he didn't like sex. Wasn't interested in the feel of a woman. *Stay on your side of the bed.*

Instead of me moving in, I moved to Beaverton, a stone's throw from where he lived. We'd been dating since shortly after I moved to Madras, and I figured things would keep progressing when I was closer and we could spend more time together. I hoped he wouldn't need to go to the strip club so frequently once he had a real woman around. But I was wrong of course.

He told me he liked it better before my move over the mountain, when I only came around once every couple of weeks. *Can we go back to that? It's too much, having you here all the time.* I tell him I'd understand if he was sleeping with one of the strippers, but I know how hands off he is with me and so I was sure that wasn't the problem. The truth was, he wanted me for show. An intermittent trophy. A steady girlfriend as a front to keep whatever secrets he had hidden from the world. *Thanks, but no thanks. There's another guy in line.*

The night Thumbs and I split, I went home to drink a case of beer alone on the front stoop of my apartment. A neighbor, the guy from upstairs, asked me if I was okay. *Where's Thumbs?* I tell him we've broken up. *Didn't he just help you move in? I swear I saw him just the other day.* I cried in front of this stranger – this neighbor who was more curious than he should be about the drunk woman crying on the stoop.

The next morning, hungover and bleary eyed, trying to get ready for work, I looked at myself in the mirror. I looked as horrible as I felt. I was tired of the relationship cycle. Waiting to be loved. Drowning my misery in more misery. I decided to opt out of it; to simply not do it anymore. I made a conscious decision that I wouldn't call the next man in line. I vowed to refuse the urge to head to the bar for a distraction. For once, I would keep to myself. I'd keep on track to make my own way, and the first step was to focus on not walking out on my job at the call center until I had my insurance license in hand.

Then the neighbor appeared again. I couldn't remember his name, although he'd introduced himself a few times. I'm terrible with names. He nervously stood on my front step and invited me to lunch. I was hungry. My brother hadn't paid rent yet, so I didn't exactly have money for food. I'd spent the last of it on beer. I agreed to lunch but was careful to announce that we'd only be going as friends. Neighbors.

The neighbor was nice. Different from the others in a way I couldn't put my finger on. He had a job, which was always a plus, and didn't live with his parents. He collected action figures instead of notches on his belt. He seemed lonely; almost as lonely as me. It wasn't the first time I'd talked to a neighbor and not remembered their name, but it is the first time I'd had a neighbor who wanted to be my friend. Besides, he didn't remember my name either, so we were even from the start.

We got to know each other slowly over episodes of *Survivor* and *CSI: Las Vegas*. I finally discovered and found a way to remember that this neighbor's name was Keith. I could hear his door open when he went outside to smoke, and so I'd take Goliath out for a walk whenever I heard him milling around on his patio. If I took Goliath out for a walk any other time, Keith would hear my door open so he'd come out too. We talked over the rail while I avoided the little girl who kept breaking into my apartment.

At some point in our neighborly friendship he kissed me. I don't remember when, exactly, but I do remember telling him that I'd decided to not dive into anything. I held back. Our clothes stayed on and for weeks we went on mild dates like middle school students with a curfew.

Then, as it always does, money got tighter, a guy started staring at me through the windows of my ground floor apartment and I became simultaneously terrified that I was going to get evicted for missing the rent, and be stalked by this peeping tom forever. Keith, had somehow become my boyfriend despite my best efforts at keeping him at arm's length. He moved in when his lease was up and helped me keep the roof over my head. *I was paying the rent upstairs anyway. It's all the same to me.*

I vowed then that with Keith, things were going to be different. And for the last eleven years, it has been.

My instant messenger beeps. A screen name I knew years before appears on the screen. It's someone I loved in another life. Someone who kept me sane amongst the insanity. A friend who happened to call at the very moment I gazed up at the trees, ready to hang myself. He says life has changed and he wants to be friends again. I'm excited. Ecstatic. Breathless with joy at his return. So happy, in fact, that I tell Keith all about it.

The messages continue for a couple of weeks and then something new. This friend is coming to town. Wants to go to dinner. Meet Keith and catch up, like the old days. He's missed me and wants to make sure I'm okay. I assure him I am. We've just bought a house, we've gotten engaged. I'm working and making a living again.

We set a date, and something comes up. Keith can't make it, has to work late. *Don't worry about it. I'll see you later tonight. Have fun with your friend.* We meet up and go out for sandwiches. Casual. Nothing to see here. I hope Keith's plans will change, that he'll be able to meet up, but he can't get out of whatever catastrophe is going on at the office. I take my friend home, to our house for a while. Show him around the life that I live. He hugs me and wishes me well, glad to see that I've made it far beyond the hell that I'd lived before.

Then the friend appears again. On my phone. In my computer. He was wrong. He misses me. We had talked about being together one day, before life changed. Before things were different. I loved him once, and part of me loved him still. But he was still the same ghost that I left behind, haunting the home of another woman, popping pills to try to numb his own pain. *Not too many, just enough to get by.* Drowning his misery in more misery. My understanding of his situation confirmed when his wife called. *Keep away. I'll shoot you. Blast you full of holes until you're dead.*

Keith didn't deserve to be dragged down into that world, to have a woman unsure of which side of the fence her feet should stand. Keith said if I stayed, I'd have to let the friend go. It didn't matter if he'd rescued me before, he wasn't rescuing me now. I was sober and scared, scared of losing the life I'd built. Scared of giving up the man who loved only me for a man who'd only love me when it was convenient.

The decision was made and ties were cut. He'd been my closest friend once, this phantom voice that floated in and out of the phone receiver. He'd convinced me to put down the rope and face life again when I was ready to tie a noose and give up. I loved him once, and a part of me loves him still, but not enough to ruin what I have now.

I still think of him. The phantom. I'm sure he thinks of me, too. Neither of us pick up the phone.

Hench~~man~~
Hench~~woman~~
Hench~~person~~
Life Insurance Sales

When I returned to Portland from Madras, I was resolved that I would only use the call center gig at the bank as a stop-gap while I got my insurance license. A union-based insurance company I'd never heard of was willing to take me on as a sales person, provided I could get my license, and so I rubbed the last of my pennies together and got myself enrolled in insurance school.

From the start, the insurance setup was weird. There was a school, sort of. It was in a building, a place that I could drive to and check in. For the license, I was required to have a certain number of hours of monitored schooling and pass a series of tests. In theory it made sense, but in practice it all felt like a sham.

I walked into the "classroom" that first day with my stack of insurance books to find another world inhabited by a sea of cubicles. These ones weren't the spacious three foot by three foot islands of pleasure I was used to. Instead, they were about two feet wide and eighteen inches deep. Like study cubes from a pre-1990s library. There was one other warm body in the room, and he wasn't an instructor. Another student. I think he was taking a nap.

It didn't take long for me to discover that my insurance licensing requirements weren't all they were cracked up to be. Monitored learning simply meant that there was someone at the front desk who could vouch for my being on the property. And the tests were simply sheets of paper with multiple choice questions on them that I self-graded. I did have to turn them in to have the grades verified by the desk-sitter in the end, I think. But most of the time I was at the "Insurance School" I was trying to not drool on my textbooks while any other students played FreeCell on their laptops or caught up on some sleep.

The week I got my license in the mail, I put in my notice at the bank. I was done talking on the phone (or so I thought). I was absolutely exhausted by the cycle of encouraging people to get into more debt, and then trying to beat monthly payments out of them. *I see you have a $906,000 mortgage, and you're two months behind. How are you going to resolve that? By the way – have you considered taking out a home equity loan?*

My first day on the job in insurance was another eye-opening experience. The building that housed the company I was working for was a beautiful, all glass office building. Not a skyscraper, but many stories high. It gleamed in the morning sun and made me feel like I was finally going places. I hopped onto the elevator and when the lift doors opened they revealed to me... a sparsely decorated generic office. The conference room was jam packed with other new sales reps, and I seem to remember there weren't enough chairs for everyone. That day, I got an inspiring pep-talk from Roger, who assured us all that he had made so much money in insurance that he didn't even need to be there that day – he was purely speaking to us for our own good. I was sorted into a training group under a charismatic young guy who seemed like he could sell pants to a gorilla. I was handed boatloads of paperwork. And that was it.

Well, not quite. I think before we left that day, we each had to verify that we had cell phones, and then we spent two hours using our personal lines to "warm call" hundreds of people until we had set up enough appointments for our team leads to work the next few days. For those of you who don't know, a warm call is *completely* different from a cold call because, although the people still have no idea who you are or why you're calling, and you're likely interrupting their dinner by trying to convince them to invite a stranger into their house to sell them something – although all that is still true – they brought the call on themselves by checking a little box on a paper provided to them by their banking establishment or union. Weeks, or months, or sometimes years before, they had asked for more information about a free life insurance policy and while we'd given them radio silence since then, by God, we were available to beat them over the head with it now.

And so, I joined a band of traveling insurance salespeople. We had a home office but only went there for meetings where we were told how great we were for getting out in the field. Most of the time, I was in my car driving from appointment to appointment, knocking on strangers' doors and asking them if they'd thought about what was going to happen to their families when they die. I sold some policies, gave limited one-year thousand-dollar life policies away by the bucket full, and lived the life of a nomad. My sales territory was often hundreds of miles from home, and so for a while I didn't see much of Keith aside from coming home broke and tired while I waited for my commission checks to roll in.

I did have an opportunity to sell a giant policy. A monster policy that would have kept us fed for a while. I'd somehow been given the opportunity to cover some ground in Portland (I'm pretty sure I was picking up my trainer's appointments because he frequently couldn't be located). I pulled up to a beautiful historic craftsman style home. I was greeted at the stained glass front door and ushered into a foyer. Yes. A house with an actual foyer. It had been meticulously tiled by someone with an eye for reclaimed flooring. The house was empty aside from a middle-aged man and myself. He led me into his kitchen, we sat down at a round table that could have served King Arthur, his knights, and any women that might be hanging on.

The second I got myself settled in the high-back chair, the man looked across the table at me and said, "I need to take out a three million dollar policy on my wife."

Now, for all you people not in insurance sales, it's often perfectly legal to take out an insurance policy for someone else. Depending on the state, the insurance company, and the underwriter, it's often no big deal. The insured may not even have to fill out any paperwork. Meaning, conceivably, you could take out a giant policy against someone without them knowing a damn thing about it (this is untrue if the underwriter requires a physical – then you've got to find a way to get the insured to the doctor).

For the insurance agent, it often doesn't matter what you're asking for. We're here to serve you. Because that's how we get paid. But there was something off about this guy, hanging out alone in the middle of the day in a giant house, asking for three million dollars' coverage in under ninety seconds of meeting me. He gave me the heebie jeebies. I gave him the basic information, told him I'd have to go back to my office to figure out policy amounts, and then I told my trainer I wasn't comfortable writing the policy.

But what about the money? The commission on that will be great. But what if this guy offs his wife six months after he pulls the policy? *Not our problem.*

I passed on selling that policy, although I'm sure my trainer went back and filed the forms for the guy. I wrote a lot of other policies though, for a lot of interesting people. My favorite client was an elevator repair guy. I sat down with him, his wife, and his daughter and gave them my little spiel about how important it is to have a life insurance policy in place when you have a family. He nodded, and asked me to start telling him what he qualified for.

Elevator repair is one of the most dangerous professions a person can have. It turns out, it's not just the drop that kills you. There's the threat of electrocution from improperly installed, maintained, or tampered-with electrical systems. You've got the possibility of being crushed if something shifts, or if the neighboring elevator doesn't get shut off (why should we inconvenience our residents while you work on elevator #1 when we have a perfectly good elevator #2 right next door?). There's falling tools. There's unstable heavy equipment. There's the fact that no one can see you working, so they forget you're up there and start mashing buttons on the keypad.

So, he bought a policy. He already had a couple of others, but he held no illusions to the threats on his life provided by his profession. When I asked him why he kept at it – he'd been an elevator repair person for many years – he told me simply that when he started working fresh out of trade school, he made more than a doctor might. And now, having survived the industry for so long, he made much, much more than that.

The elevator repair man wasn't living opulently despite his pay grade. Their house doesn't stand out in my memory of being greater than average. They had regular family cars. Children's art on the walls. This man wasn't raking in the money to keep up with societal appearances – he was socking money away to make sure his family would be okay without him. He'd started a family with his wife when they were young, and he made the decision to put his life on the line to make sure his children would grow up in a secure home. The concept gave me pause.

Who was *I* working for?

I'd gotten into insurance sales because I was tired of being at the mercy of someone else. I liked the idea of setting my own hours (even if it meant I was working all the hours). I enjoyed the freedom of not being tied to a desk. I made a friend, Elise, and we had a riot of a time couch surfing while we traveled around asking people, *But what if you die?* I wasn't working to cement a future for anyone, and to this day I'm still not, although it would be nice to have a nest egg one day. I had been simply working to get from day to day, until the next "big thing" came along.

At the time I was selling policies, I was also finishing writing my first novel. A contemporary romance, *Age/Sex/Location: Love is just a click away*, was going to be my ticket out of the working world. I was sure of it.

A BUYER OF LOVE

Now that I'm settled in a relationship that's not lopsided, I realize how far I've gone in pursuit of someone who thinks I have worth. I look back on my sea of lost loves and view the debris of myself floating on the waves. I turn to Keith as he sleeps. I, of course, am up at 3:00 a.m. I tally the things that I know I've done in the pursuit of having someone who will simply stay with me.

If I love you, I'll cook for you. Clean for you. Bake you cookies on a Tuesday just because. I'll sit with you. Stand with you. Keep you company when I'd rather be alone. I'll do your homework for you. Cover your shifts if we happen to work together. Call in sick for you if we don't. I'll lie for you. Give up friends for you. Ignore my family if you think it's best. I'll live with you, or without you, whichever you prefer at the time.

I won't call the cops when we're arguing. Even if you throw my keys on the roof so I can't come in and can't leave. Even if bruises are left behind. I won't nag if you're jobless for whatever reason, even if that reason is just that you know your parents will take care of you while you wait for them to die so you can inherit their fortune.

I'll support you financially, if I can, and be broke with you if I can't. I'll pretend we're just friends if your other girlfriend is nearby. I'll even buy you a present if you decide to marry her instead of me. I'll hold a camera and tell you all to smile on your wedding day, frowning into the viewfinder "to get a better shot" even if all I see is you looking back at me like you don't know that I'm dying inside. I'll go on a date with the friend you set me up with to cover our indiscretions, and pretend to have a good time.

I'll move for you. Across the nation, across the border, across town. Distance doesn't matter. I'll move closer to you. Farther away. Whatever fits the storyline of our romance. I'll plead with your superiors, plead with the landlord, plead with whoever's in charge to not kick us out. Not let us go. Keep a roof over our head and food in our bellies, even if it's only ramen cut with macaroni and cheese (a delicacy called Stoner Surprise). I'll make you a quilt while you're in jail. Keep it to myself when you spend all the grocery money and I'm left to search the back of the pantry for something to eat alone on Thanksgiving.

I'll tolerate other partners. Men or women, what's your pleasure? I won't bat an eye when you hand them my rent money. I'll keep a secret bank account, filter money there so when you've given away everything you know we have, I still have something to keep the car full of gas. I'll find another job. A second. A third. It'll be okay.

I'll worry when you don't call, but I'll give you your space. I'll be glad when you arrive again, whether it's days or weeks later. I'll act like nothing's happened, like there isn't a gap in your life I know nothing about. I'll make up a story for you to tell our friends, if we have any. I won't hold a grudge, not too much of one anyway. I'll keep my resentments to myself, and find a way to make sure they aren't your fault.

I'll let you touch me, even when my skin crawls. Do all kinds of weird favors depending on your fetish. Bend and move even when it hurts. Do my best to not complain. I'll marry you, or date you forever. Or just be friends with benefits if that's your thing. I'll be committed, or consider revolving partners. Open marriage, closed marriage, isn't it all the same in the end? Get you some strange, get me some, too.

I'll tell you stories. Write you a poem. Sing you a song. Dance for you. Lie with you. Anything to keep your attention. I'll be a puppet with strings you pull, or a paperweight holding you down. Tell me what you need and I'll do it a thousand times. Even when I'm tired. Even when I hate you. Even when I wish I would die so I wouldn't have to feel the heartbreak any more. *I'll die tomorrow – too many other things to do today.*

After my divorce, before I meet Keith, while I'm dating a handful of men in rotation, I think back on Ryan. When we were kids, I chatted with him on a green screen in a chatroom I had to have a phone number to dial into. We ended up going to the same summer camp. I liked him and he liked me. A week of friendship, then we went home and I decided not to use that chatroom any more. My anonymity lost, I couldn't be myself with him online anymore.

A couple of years later, in middle school, another room online, I strike up a conversation with a guy. He's local. He's interesting. Somehow, I convince a parent to take me to the mall to meet him. I don't remember a chaperone beyond the car ride. Maybe it's an axe murderer. A grownup disguised. Nope, it's Ryan. We have lunch, talk about summer camp so long ago. Part ways again and I abandon his online persona once more.

After high school, the summer between graduation and what would be my failure as a college student, I run into him again. He's working at RadioShack with some friends. I start to party with them. Ryan is into me, so I make out with his friends. He's the nicest guy I know. He does take me home once, to meet his family. They're normal. Supportive. He's told them about me. He kisses me once. I'm drunk at the time but not so drunk that I don't remember. He holds me in his arms like he doesn't want me to leave. I think he could love me, but he's the kind of guy that treats you right. What would I do with him? I stop calling. Lose touch. Move away so the party will stop.

Then, I'm divorced. Back in Oregon. *Back in the States*, many people say, apparently oblivious to Hawaii being a part of this grand union. I should call Ryan. He's the one I should have been with this entire time. I find him online. Not hard after all the practice I've had bumping into him on accident.

He's married. Has kids. A mortgage and two cars. He's in love with his life, but glad that I called. He'll pop in to chat where I work a couple of times, we'll reminisce about strange moments in our adolescence. Stare at each other across the counter and all I'll see is the life I could have had if I hadn't been so drawn to people who couldn't love me. I don't know what he thinks of me. He doesn't say.

MANAGER OF THINGS

You're stupid to think that some guy is going to marry you and stick with you. That's what my supervisor at the insurance company said when I announced that Keith had asked me to marry him.

Once upon a time, Keith said that I was complex. That convincing me of something takes a multi-level, long term, gentle approach. I'm here to tell you though, that there's a simple, one-step way to jumpstart my decision making. Just tell me I'm stupid and can't do something.

The way the insurance agency was structured, my supervising agent got a percentage of every policy I wrote. My success was his success. After being told how dumb I was for thinking someone might want to spend their life with me, I decided on the spot that this guy wasn't going to benefit from my hard work anymore. I stopped writing policies and within a week I was turning in any company-owned materials I still had in my possession.

I was proud of myself for dumping the gig. I'd been working a lot of hours. Spending too much money on gas and time on the road. The one thing I loved about my job was hanging out with my new sister-in-arms, Elise, but time would show that she wasn't going anywhere. Well, she was going everywhere, but she wouldn't lose my phone number.

And so, after just a few months of being an insurance agent, I found myself unemployed. Bills were due, I'd been borrowing money from Keith to cover them between paychecks. I looked out on the job horizon and the only openings that called my name were more call-center jobs. I knew if I went back to the gray on gray world of cubicles that I'd die inside. I decided to take my chances with a temp agency. They promised me a new gig every week, if I was up to it.

It took a few days for my first assignment to come in. They told me it was for a job working at a reception desk, and I told them I didn't want to do it. *I don't want to talk on the phone.* The recruiter told me that it was just one job. In a week or two, they'd find me something else to do. Besides, it would open me up to a different kind of phone work and that would look like a step up on my resume.

I arrived at the address on the assignment sheet and parked just outside the roped off lot. I punched the number of the agency office. There had to be a problem with the address. I was sitting just outside of a fast food joint. *No, the address is correct. They just opened and need someone to answer the phone.* I didn't want to be on the phone, and I didn't want to work fast food. My recruiter told me I had to work at least two days while they found another candidate. I sighed in resignation.

That first shift was insane. A family had moved up to Oregon from Texas and brought their southern-based restaurant franchise with them. People lined up for hours to hit the drive through. The phone was ringing off the hook as I set my stuff down on the narrow steel desk in the manager's office (two tables plopped down in the middle of the kitchen). It didn't stop ringing. That first day I answered the phone, non-stop, for twelve hours. The people calling were asking for driving directions from places all over the state. The scene inside the restaurant was a blur – people were struggling to keep up with the thousands of customers rolling through. It was intense. Exciting. Plus, they gave me free food.

I called the temp agency back and told them I'd finish out the two-week commitment. Two weeks later, the gig was extended through the end of the month. I performed well; my familiarity with life on a three-minute script kept up with the phones and I could take care of the few customer complaints that came in without having to ask anyone else for help.

The franchise owners decided that I was worth keeping on. They told me they did have an actual office, just up the road, and they needed an office manager to keep track of paperwork and support the restaurant management staff. They bought out my contract with the temp agency, and I'd end up working for them for four years.

"Working" isn't the right word. I committed myself to the expansion of a burger empire. I loved being there and found myself spending most of my waking hours poring over spreadsheets, processing new hire paperwork, and routing much less frequent phone calls to the appropriate parties. I excelled. I worked mostly by myself in the small office. I'd do errands for the owners if they were around, and dive into mountains of data and paperwork if they weren't. The longer I stayed, the more integrated into the running of things I became. In less than a year I was doing more than my job description could possibly cover; I was assisting with (or simply the only one doing) payroll, human resources, got the stores into state compliance for OSHA, and helped edit and update the training materials for employees company-wide.

I was being groomed for more responsibility, and rewards, than I dreamed a fast-food job could possibly offer. I trekked to Oklahoma for a company convention that dwarfed any other convention I've ever attended, both in mass of attendance and evangelical dedication to the "tots or fries?" cause. I was bought in. Sold. Signed, sealed, delivered. I could see myself engaged with this company and its people for decades. I loved it, and for a time, it seemed it loved me.

We were all riding a pretty huge wave. Our little restaurant was breaking national sales records. When a second restaurant was built, the results were similarly incredible. The golden goose had come. My fellow managers and I marveled at how lucky we were to be a part of something so simply great. Just when we got used to how good things were, everything would get inexplicably better.

Then, three years in, the bubble burst. A third location opened during the same time that Keith and I got married. Prior to the wedding, things were still trending up. I had voiced some reservations about the location that they'd decided to put the third store, but the other two sites had done so well that everyone was convinced the location didn't matter. *If you build it, they'll find the drive-thru.*

I was away from work for about a month. First, for the wedding of the ages (red carpet, steak and lobster, and an awards ceremony that made us all feel like celebrities for a day). Then, Keith and I took a luxurious week-long cruise down the coast of Mexico. On our way home, we both caught a mutant international cruise-line flu that had us both green and spewing for a couple of weeks. When I returned, the landscape was horrifically different.

The new restaurant opening was a flop. It probably would have been okay, as far as restaurant openings go, but everyone had prepared for a much higher volume of customers than showed up. Expenditures were bursting at the seams without the sales needed to back them up. They'd hired too many people, bought too much food, spent too much time and money on traffic control. Rather than being bursting to the gills for months, sales trickled in. As emotionally invested as we all were, it was a blow to our egos and our confidence.

My bosses, the franchise owners, took the opening of the third site hard. The strain on their personal lives was clear as they grappled with suddenly not being the golden franchisees. Unfortunately, their response to the matter at hand was swift and unforgiving. Within a few weeks, I discovered that the empire we'd built was crumbling. My peers were let go rapid-fire until only a couple of us original employees remained. Nobody's jobs were safe. I started crumbling under the pressure to do more. Everything I did was scrutinized, and any input I'd previously had on running the business dissolved. A few months later, I was dying under the strain. I'd go home crying because the demands were so great, and all the recognition I'd known previously had been pulled off the table.

I decided to stand up for myself and ask for a raise. If they were going to continue to expect me to push fifty hour weeks, at least they could bump my salary. I pulled a list of my responsibilities, cross referenced those with the pay scale of the other managers (those working inside the restaurant), and called a meeting with the bosses. They did offer me a small raise, but it wasn't what I'd hoped for. Not enough for me to keep working myself to death.

Around the time that I was bargaining for a better return on my labor investment, I also got some interest in my first novel, *Age/Sex/Location: Love is just a click away.* The contemporary romance had been passed over by several publishers, but suddenly I found myself turning down a publishing contract from one company, and accepting a contract from Brighton Publishing. When Brighton Publishing and I reached an agreement, my decision was made. I was going to stop working for other people and focus on working for myself.

I learned a lot working with the editors, artists, and press folk at Brighton Publishing, and a few months after I quit being an office manager I held my first book in my arms. Freshly inked, encased in a glossy cover, it was like holding a newborn baby for the first time. I breathed something into the world and it manifested itself in paperback. I'd always written, from the time I was a kid. But now that I'd showed it to someone, and they thought it was worth selling, I was hooked on the author bug.

Most of my time as an office manager is spent alone. I receive hundreds of emails a day, but otherwise my office is my domain. My desk is the only one in the building with a window, unless you count the pass-through that connects my work area to the office behind my desk. My grand window view is of two empty parking spaces out front, and a blank corner of the warehouse across the lot. There's a giant pot of plants just outside the door that I watch die in the afternoon sun. I've killed about three hundred dollars' worth of plants in that pot in the three years I've been here. I'm a great office manager, but I suck at keeping potted plants alive.

One of the side-projects I've been assigned as an office manager is figuring out how to get into compliance with safety regulations without sending our insurance rates soaring. The first part of the project is relatively easy; research the regulations, figure out our risk for dangerous situations (What could possibly go wrong in a restaurant? What with the knives, boiling oil, slippery floors, hot grills and all.) and create some documents to outline what we can do to make the state, the insurance company, and our employees all relatively happy. Read, type, print. Check.

Step two of this project is a little scarier. I've got to package up this new safety program and deliver it to the managers and employees. It's not as simple as sending an email that says, *Do this.* No, the whole thing needs to be brought into the restaurants as an active dialogue so that we can fix things that aren't working as quickly as possible. So how do we do that? Oh, I have a great idea. How about I use a segment of the manager meetings, employee meetings, and orientations to speak about this safety stuff? Nods all around.

Never mind that I haven't done any type of public speaking since high school when I probably read notes from a book report aloud from my seat. Never mind the fact that I really don't know what I'm doing, and none of the changes I'm suggesting we implement are wanted or asked for. Let's just not worry about the fact that talking about safety, risk assessment, and insurance are three of the most boring things on the planet. Let's not take any of that into consideration.

This is where I discover that I cry during the first five minutes of any public speaking engagement. It doesn't matter the topic. Let's take a look at what happens when I stand up in front of a group of twenty managers to talk about enforcing the non-slip shoe policy, shall we?

Hello everyone. There is a pregnant pause while I realize that my eyes are welling up. I take a few deep breaths. Everyone is looking at me like I'm going to tell them that the President was just shot. *Today I am going to remind you again (sniffle) that you cannot let your employees wear canvas sneakers at the fry station.*

I sniffle and wipe a trailing tear from my cheek. *These are teenagers, working in grease, spilling it on the* (sniffle, tear) *ground and then flailing around in it. Teenagers are* (silent gasp for air) *stupid, let's face it. Make them wear approved shoes or* (sniffle) *OSHA is going to write us up again.*

I stand there, breathing deeply, gaining some control over my tear ducts. Everyone else looks up at me, trying to figure out why I'm so broken up over a bunch of dumb kids who think NSF safety shoes don't look cool with their uniforms. Someone has a question, and by now I'm gathered up enough that I'm able to answer it without the aid of a Kleenex. The more back and forth we have, the more words I'm able to string together without sniffling. Eventually, it turns into a decent presentation.

You might think that this is just early jitters, and you'd be right. The problem is, years later when I'm standing in front of a classroom full of aspiring authors who all want to hear about my novel, *Adaline*, the same scene will play out again. At some point, I decide I'm going to just start telling people that I'll come talk to their group as long as they ask me questions about starving children and homeless puppies for the first five minutes so that I can shed my introductory tears over worthy issues. Then we can get on with the speaking topic at hand like normal human beings.

FREELANCE
WOMAN OF WONDER

When you publish your first book, you try to be humble about it. Although it's your baby, and you know that you've put your all into it, you know it isn't likely to sell a million copies right off. *I'll be okay if it only sells a few thousand.*

Well, it's not that easy. I won't go into all the back-end nuts and bolts of publishing (unless you want to chat about it – in which case, e-mail me), but as a new author with no following, selling a few thousand copies is a herculean effort. At the time of this writing, I've published or self-published six books and I'm still working on hitting that goal of a few thousand sold.

There are people who will tell you this. They'll congratulate you on finishing your first book, and then tell you to keep your day job just in case it doesn't work out. If you happen to be fortunate enough to meet other authors who will be candid with you, they may even tell you that endeavoring to support yourself with writing is a fool's journey. I talked to these people after I quit my job and was sitting at home waiting for royalty checks to come in.

The good news is, royalty checks did come. The bad news is, the payments from that first book were only enough to buy a laptop from Groupon, and a Cannon printer on clearance at Best Buy. Not exactly the financial windfall that I'd hoped for. I had to find something else to fill the days so that I could leave my publisher alone (they don't like being emailed every thirty minutes for sales updates), and I needed to make some money. But I wouldn't give up on the writing, I'd simply expand it. Through a myriad of Google searches and web-referrals, I ended up finding a handful of sites that would pay me to write online content for them.

Freelance web writing isn't the same as novel writing, the same way driving a taxi isn't the same as racing in the Indie 500. The basics are the same, sure. Both drivers have a steering wheel and gas pedal. Both writers have a keyboard and access to a litany of vocabulary. But that's where the similarities end. Writing freelance was both easier and more maddening than novel writing. On the one hand, I started making real money with my writing. Credit card payment money. Grocery money. Mortgage money. On the other hand, I had to write several articles, blog posts, and filler copy pieces a day.

To make it work, I was accepting writing gigs for things I had no clue about. I wrote about sandwiches, health, beauty, parenting, local events, national events, cars, cabinetry, homemaking, personal care, finance, sports, food, relationships, and so much more that I don't even remember. Churning out three to six articles a day, I would sometimes get an email from someone who enjoyed my work and I'd have no idea what they were talking about. I'd have to look up my own article to remember what I'd written.

It didn't take me long to realize that churning out short dribble pieces for the internet was squashing my writing ability overall. It was stunting my vocabulary (frilly words don't hit those search engine optimization keys very well), it was taking up huge blocks of research time that I wasn't getting paid for, and while it was getting me primed to hit a set word-count of writing each day, the words were being wasted on things like how to take care of cracked feet and oxidized paint. Deep down I knew that I had more stories to tell, and I couldn't let a tidal wave of infomercial-type material get in the way.

My problem was surreal. I wanted to be a paid writer, and that's exactly what I was! I was writing and people or companies were cutting me checks. But I wasn't getting paid to write what I wanted to write. My passion was not writing about cabinetry hinges for an afternoon and then turning around to learn about the proper way to service a hot water heater (flush the sediment out every six months, and that heater will last forever). But I couldn't very well walk away from the money either. What kind of crazy person would give up being paid to write when they wanted to be paid to write?

What I did instead was shift my focus. In essence, I dumped the online gigs in favor for more personal projects. I was still doing freelance work, but I set my own per-word rate and chose topics that mattered to me. I gave up the gunshot approach to writing everything I won a bid on, and instead focused on writing about the paintball industry, which is something I knew a little about and had some interest in. I selected a couple of reliable clients who offered reasonable deadlines so I had time to breathe, and then I focused primarily on doing press releases and product reviews that could be written via some self-made templates so I didn't have to think quite so hard to put the work together.

As a small business person, I learned a lot from the freelance writing gigs. The first thing I learned was that each word I write has value (no less than $0.10 per word, thank you). As a writer, I learned that there are people out there who are reading all sorts of things. They're reading to learn, to escape, to make sure they're keeping up with their neighbors. They want to be entertained, and they hope to read something that tells them they're on the right track for having a fulfilling life. As a novelist, I learned that the stories I had to tell could fill those same needs.

I haven't done much freelance work since my life got turned upside-down in 2013 (more on that later). But doing it was, and is, something that helped to shape my writing. Through it, I met and interviewed people who were doing amazing things with their lives. I continue to be inspired by several of them.

Keith has been supportive of my writing from the very beginning. He finds it funny and engaging, or at least pretends to think that in order to have occasional adult sexy-time. At any rate, he puts on a good show of being encouraging and proud of my written words. One of his grand displays of affection was to build us a home-office that would make Stephen King jealous.

During my freelance days, I spent a good eight hours a day in the office. My desk looked out over our driveway, across the front yards of our neighbors' houses and onto the train tracks that crawled around behind our neighborhood. The way the window was situated, the sun would stream in, its welcome rays warming me as I sat in my bucket-seat office chair (five-point harness not included) churning out articles about *Why You Should Work at Home*.

It was bliss. Until Mrs. Neighbor noticed me.

The Neighbors were basically good neighbors. Their house was nicer than ours. It was cleaner than ours. It was more "suburban" than ours, owing to my desire to be a micro-farmer coupled with my inability to keep plants alive. They were nice people who had many of the same interests as us. We were the same age. We liked similar games, music, and activities. We should have been great friends. Except.

Except that when I would sit, sunning my pajama-clad self in my perfect office window while I was trying to find just the right way to phrase, *You probably can't fix that HVAC problem yourself,* for a piece I was writing, Mrs. Neighbor would enter her front yard. She'd see me sitting there, gazing out my window. She'd wave. I'd give her a smile or a wave because, hey, I'm a pleasant person. Then she'd pantomime something to me. I'd shake my head and get back to work. Mrs. Neighbor would take this to mean that I wanted her to come over to hang out.

When she came over, I'd say hello and explain that I was working and really needed to get back to it. Somehow, she'd make her way into the house and sit down on the couch. *Oh, I know all about deadlines. I have a lot of those with my acting work.*

After a few weeks of these pop-in visits, it became clear that she believed I honestly had nothing to do, and I was a reclusive shut-in who needed to be socialized. I'm sure that in her kind, Christian heart, she was doing me a favor by showing me how wonderful it would be to have a best friend who lived twelve feet outside my door. We could be best friends and hang out all day while we discussed the merits and pitfalls of being moms in the entertainment industry.

No, thank you.

I stopped responding to her waves through the window. If I saw even a flutter of movement coming from outside the window, I'd lean forward in my chair and make a great attempt at being suddenly engrossed in my work.

Mrs. Neighbor would simply come over and knock on the door anyway. She could see I was home, and apparently as I looked sternly at my computer screen, I looked troubled.

I told her I was busy, I really did. Still, she'd invite me over for lunch, or a movie, or to have a midday glass of wine. I turned down all but her most enticing offers (sometimes a midday glass of wine *is* nice). The handful of times I abandoned my work for her company over the years that we lived next door to one another, her visits became immediately more frequent.

So, I stopped answering the door. This did not work. For one thing, she had to walk past my office window to make it to the door so she knew I was home. I thought if I had my headphones on *and* I looked terribly intent on my work *and* I fought the urge to respond to the banging sounds on the door, that she'd understand I was busy. Wrong. Mrs. Neighbor stopped going to the door altogether and would simply stand outside the window until she was sure I'd noticed her.

As I am not an aggressive person, and I have immense difficulty with confrontation, I will admit that there were days when I was hard up on a deadline or feeling particularly "in the groove" in which I would park my car around the corner, draw the shades, turn off the lights, and do my best to make it appear that no one was home. I only did it a couple of times, and I'm not proud of it. Hiding in my own house doesn't make me a Great American Writer.

I allowed Mrs. Neighbor to ruin the deep love I had for my perfect office. My husband built my desk, storage cubbies, shelves, and footlocker with his own hands. He lovingly installed and painted every piece of furniture that I asked for. But having a woman hovering on the other side of the glass, looking in on me like a zoo animal that needed to be tamed and socialized "for the greater good" ruined my ability to enjoy it. The dread of her presence made me want an office space away from home. A place where I could go to work like a normal person and be left alone.

As it turns out, I'd end up with way more office and work than I could handle.

LIFE COACH

In the midst of my change from corporate to private life, my mother called me with some unsettling news. Her then-husband, Jay, was parading around their apartment with a butcher knife, plotting the murder of the property manager. She needed me to drive the three hours to pick her up and move her out before things escalated any further.

Although Keith and I had long had reservations about Jay, neither of us were prepared for the tidal wave of information that would follow that call. My mom had been living in fear and seclusion for years, unable to find a way to communicate her plight to us so that we might rescue her. It wasn't until his anger finally put someone else in danger that she fled to a nearby family member's house and asked for help putting distance between herself and the madman she'd married.

I made the trek back to Madras, where Mom and Jay had been living, and escorted her back to her apartment just long enough to pick up a box of her medications while Jay looked on. I made sure he knew that I'd already notified my former coworkers at the county Sheriff's Office of the situation, and if he made a wrong move that the deputies would rain down on the apartment. Sometimes, it pays to have a work history that includes a wide variety of support.

Within a few hours, I'd brought my mother back to live with Keith and me. We spent the next few days scouring thrift stores and discount racks for new clothes for her, got her set up with her own space in an unused bedroom, and I began the task of teaching her how to live on her own.

In the years since I'd moved out on my own, Mom had become a product of the industrial medical system. Following my parents' divorce, she'd been found to be too anxious, depressed, and emotionally unstable to work and had been labeled as disabled by her medical staff and the federal government. She'd been systematically supported and repelled by a series of doctors who overmedicated her and then treated her as a pill-seeking patient. She had therapists who seemed to give her permission to let go of basic life skills, and enabled her to use her mental illness as an excuse for even the smallest things. I hardly recognized her by the time I brought her into our home. She'd transformed from a bright and capable young woman who took on the world without breaking a sweat, to a middle-aged morbidly obese person with the physical and mental capabilities of a child.

Somehow, I managed to sidestep any feelings of guilt from my mom's physical and mental condition. It seems like the kind of thing that I'd take on as my own doing, but as much as I like to burden myself with other people's problems, I knew that I'd never been in a position to save my mom from herself before. Where she'd landed in her life wasn't a product of my doing, but I knew that I could help her if she was ready to help herself.

Although the few months she lived with us were often frustrating for Keith and I, we did our best to be patient with Mom as she relearned how to live life. After we got her clothed, the next thing I did was re-teach mom to eat food that didn't come out of a carton. I wasn't in peak physical condition myself, but Keith and I had both begun our own journey towards a more wholesome and sustainable life, and it was only a couple of weeks before my demands for change in Mom's diet started making a difference.

Beyond eating habits, it was unreal how many basic life skills my mom had lost in the years we'd been apart. Whether she asked me to, or I offered, I ended up being a coach of sorts as she worked to reclaim an adult life for herself. I encouraged her to join a gym despite her physical aches and pains, helped her to find a new doctor who was on-board with Mom taking a more whole-body approach to dealing with her type two diabetes, and helped her to reclaim the Social Security benefits that she'd lost when she married Jay.

Returning to the role of my parent's parent was difficult. She often hovered over me as I tried to work, so I took the time to help her find her own hobbies and projects to pursue so I could continue to write. She marveled at my ability to cook and bake, forgetting that she'd once run a cake decorating business from the kitchen of my childhood home. I had to remind her how to clean up after herself, and lead her back into the land of regular personal hygiene despite her long past with the phrase *cleanliness is next to Godliness*. The time was a blur of education and growth for her. It was a time of intense agitation for me.

Keith took most of the struggle with Mom in stride, listening to me whisper-rant behind closed doors and offering his condolences when I could do nothing but throw my hands in the air in frustration. He was a great support to me when I was ready to strangle the woman who was supposed to be a middle-aged adult, but who was unable to function as well as a latchkey pre-teen.

The relationship and how I viewed my mom as a functional individual was salvaged after a few months when the fog of her overmedication lifted, her confidence in leaving the house alone returned, and she began to take steps to having a life that didn't need to be chaperoned day and night. We were able to get her an apartment with another single female roommate in a nearby town, I taught her how to ride the bus (despite her early terror of the strangers on public transportation), and we got her signed up for a list of classes, support groups, and therapy sessions that would ensure she'd have professional support as she regained her independence.

At the end of the experience, my mom stated that I should take on a career in therapy, since I'd done such wonders for her. All she could see from it was the benefits to her acquisition of life skills, the boost to her self-confidence, and the relief she felt after unloading the burdens of her previous year's emotional abuse in discussions over breakfast. What she couldn't see was that although I was willing to help her, since she's my mom, I didn't *want* to help anyone. I can't separate my happiness from someone else's misery, and as much relief as she felt in that time of her life, I was slogging around a heap of unbearable burdens. I'd helped Mom because in all the years since I'd fought for my independence from her, no one (not even herself) had put in the work to improve her life since my departure. But there's no amount of money or recognition that would ever make me want to go through that again.

I hung up the pseudo-coach hat as soon as Mom moved out on her own. She'd force it back onto me again and again in the years that followed, but only for temporary stints. Now, years later, she's lived in her own apartment for several years, has formed friendships outside of our family, and has not only found a way to enjoy her independence, but has flourished after learning to make healthier life choices. I'm very proud of who she's become, but I'm even prouder that I don't have to supervise her every move anymore.

I've got other things to keep track of these days.

I'm one of those people who thinks yoga can fix anything. Well, not really anything, it can't change a flat tire. But it has given my body a sense of well-being unmatched by other exercises. So, when Mom decides to get back into shape after moving in with us, I convince her to give it a try.

We arrange the furniture in the living room and I put *Denise Austin: Fat Blasting Yoga* on the big screen. The first few minutes are okay. Mom seems upbeat and ready to go. We're stretching… we're stretching… Denise Austin sounds like she just smoked a pack of cigarettes as she's talking through the intro, which has always made me feel like I can handle this stuff no matter what. She probably just filmed this after having a cold or something, but I still imagine her lighting up before coming on set.

Then, she's done with the intro and things get moving. Mom and I bend, lift our hands over our heads, or our butts in the air per Denise's instructions. Mom starts to waver, but between Mrs. Austin's recorded encouragement and my live action prodding, Mom sticks with it.

Soon, we're both off balance, laughing at one another as we wobble on unsteady legs and try to keep up with the yoga DVD. There are times where we sit on the couch to drink water, catch our breath, and learn the poses through observation. There are few head injuries, which is incredible because it doesn't take many rapid-fire yoga poses for us to realize my big living room isn't big enough for two out of shape women to salute the sun and pretend to be trees.

We're sweaty and tired, lightheaded from giggling, and jealously mocking the svelte spandex-clad people effortlessly working through the yoga torture fest. It wouldn't take Mom long to reclaim her body from the weight that had overcome it. As time passed, we'd explore a local gym together, start completing errands around town on foot to burn calories instead of gas, and begin a new chapter in our lives together.

MOM

As a young adult, I envisioned myself as being a stay at home mom with a gaggle of children to raise. When I was married the first time, I found out that I have a condition called polycystic ovary syndrome (PCOS), which among other things makes getting pregnant a struggle. Fortunately, Marriage Round One never produced enough stability for me to try to have kids, so I had no idea how frustrating the process of childbearing would be.

When Keith and I decided to marry, we had an understanding that having children might be difficult, so we ditched the birth control months before our wedding. As we expected, nothing happened. After the wedding, we started the gargantuan task of learning everything there was to discover about the female reproductive cycle. We were up against a pretty steep learning curve though. Due to the PCOS my body was out of control. My menstrual cycle was erratic, swinging between two and a half to six weeks in length. Sometimes I missed periods for months at a time. We tried with varying degrees of intensity to get pregnant for several years.

It wasn't until we were considering in vitro fertilization that my body finally got the message. I became pregnant, and it looked like it was going to stick this time. We were excited. Well, Keith was excited. I was sick.

Out in the world of baby frenzy, people make it seem like pregnancy is a beautiful, magical time. They coo about the miracle of life, a mother-to-be's glowing skin and adorable nesting instincts. The mothers who have come before us want us to believe that every pregnancy is beautiful, sublime, and although it may be mildly uncomfortable at times, that any discomfort is swiftly forgotten once the bundle of joy arrives.

Anyone who tells you that all pregnancies are miraculous and wonderful are either bald-faced liars, or they're incredibly ignorant to how horrible such an endeavor can be. I didn't just have morning sickness, I had 24/7 sickness. My sense of smell was so out of whack that I couldn't stand the smell of most foods. I couldn't sleep, rarely ate, and generally felt like my body was being consumed by a mutant parasite from the inside-out.

I was often told by doctors, friends, and family that my misery would eventually subside. I think everyone truly believed that I'd settle into the pregnancy and start finding things to enjoy about it. But ultrasounds coupled with full bladders, strangers feeling welcome to ask about my very personal womanly condition, and the need to shop for myself and a human I'd never met (not one of my favorite endeavors) never gained any appeal to me. I began to wonder if this whole pregnancy thing was going to be worth the trouble.

All that changed six months in, but it wasn't because of hormonal fairy dust or a magic anti-nausea pill. My mom and I were out at JoAnne's Fabrics in Hillsboro, Oregon, looking for materials to make a couple of baby quilts. I hadn't had problems with incontinence, but I suddenly felt like I'd had an accident. I rushed to the bathroom and when I pulled my pants down was horrified at the amount of blood that I found. I couldn't think clearly, and although my mom was amazingly supportive, she wasn't sure what to do either. I called Keith and told him what was happening. He left work, Mom and I left the craft store, and we all raced to our house in Cornelius.

The bleeding continued, and Keith was the only person sensible enough to call a doctor. He was advised to rush me to the hospital and before I knew it, I was lying on a gurney waiting for an emergency ultrasound. Having had two previous early term miscarriages, I was sure that I was losing the baby. We were all so very relieved when we discovered that the bleeding was an anomaly, possibly caused by tissue expanding over my cervix. Everything on the ultrasound looked great, and the tech almost dropped the sex of the baby on us in her excitement (she was expecting dire results as well).

My pregnancy didn't get any easier after the bleeding scare, but I worked a lot harder to appreciate the body growing inside of me. I absolutely knew that I didn't want to lose this fetus, no matter how miserable it made me in the process. At my follow-up appointment a couple weeks later we discovered we were going to have a boy, and he appeared to be healthy as could be. We decided to name him Robert after Keith's late uncle. We'd end up calling him Bobby after the kid on the cartoon, King of the Hill. *That boy ain't right.*

When the time came to have the baby, Keith and I headed to the hospital. In the early stages of a somewhat hippy lifestyle, I wanted to have a natural birth. Labor lasted many hours, and the doctor finally gave us the option of attempting to pull Bobby out using a vacuum device, or going into surgery for a caesarian section. I wanted to try the vacuum, and the doctor agreed. He tried a couple of times to get ahold of the kid inside of me, but each time the head would appear, my son would pull back and away again. It became clear that something was wrong, and I was rushed into emergency surgery.

What they discovered was that my son had become lodged in my pelvis with the umbilical cord around his neck. After they opened me up, the doctor had to get up on the surgical table, pulling at the infant with all his might to dislodge the little bundle of goo from where he was wedged between my bones. Despite the week that followed in the hospital, me in recovery from surgery and my son in NICU recovering from injuries sustained from the various problems with his delivery, I was thankful that we had the medical staff we did that day. Without them, it is likely that either myself or my son would have died.

Another secret that many people don't talk about regarding childbirth is that a lot of people don't bond with their kids immediately. I sure didn't, and the absence of a secure emotional hold on my son made me feel like a horrible person. Not only did I not have an instant maternal instinct to love and care for this pile of squirmy goo, but a part of me resented him for putting me through so much.

Our first week as a family was segmented into thirty-minute visits to the NICU when I was feeling strong enough to walk that far. Once home, I still hadn't had the connection everyone expected, and whenever anyone offered to babysit my newborn I didn't hesitate to hand him off to them. Keith and I had just made the leap to open a paintball store a month before my son's arrival to the world, and although I understood cognitively the importance of feeding, burping, and changing my offspring, getting back to work at the shop and moving forward with business was my emotional priority.

When my son reads this passage years from now, I hope that he'll understand that his life is absolutely important to me. But those first few months, I felt like a terrible mother. I'd worked so hard to get pregnant, and had suffered through a pregnancy worse than anyone I knew. I'd wanted my child for so long, and when he arrived I simply couldn't get excited about him.

Looking back, I likely had some postpartum depression going on, and I was relying on the painkillers prescribed for the C-section wounds more than I should have. I was confused by my own lack of maternal instinct, was disappointed that motherhood wasn't the magical experience that had been advertised, and was questioning if I was even cut out for this whole Mom thing.

Now that my son is nearing his fifth birthday, I can say with certainty that despite my emotional hang-ups, I did the best I could back then. I've tried to be as open as possible with those who are curious about my birthing experience, and our family decision to not actively pursue another pregnancy. Should a pregnancy pop up on its own, we will absolutely do our best to help that child enter the world. But after multiple miscarriages and a near death experience, I feel I'm being prudent when I say that I'd rather do my best to ensure my survival for the sake of Bobby than to chase after another medical procedure that may kill me.

A crazy mom is better than no mom, after all.

Our son is four years old. He's amazingly well-behaved and adjusted, which I attribute to spending his first few years of life growing up inside of an active business. Behavioral issues with him are few and far between and are usually more comedic than dire, although there are times when I consider letting the neighbors raise him as one of their own.

I mean, he'd be close enough to visit regularly.

Potty training is a trying time in most parents' lives, and again this has been an area where our mishaps have been on the easy side of the "normal" spectrum. At the time of the telling of this story, Bobby has been potty trained for a couple of years. He has the occasional mishap after having too much to drink, and sometimes has an accident when he's too involved in a project to remember that going to the bathroom is a thing we do regularly.

A few months ago, Bobby would occasionally emerge from his trips to the bathroom with water-soaked sleeves. Dribbles down the front of his shirt. Splash patterns on his pajama pants. I didn't think much of it since he was a four-year-old washing his own hands. Water's gonna get places.

Then came the late-night visits to the bathroom. As we parents wanted Bobby to not have night time accidents, we impressed upon him that should he need to use the toilet after bedtime, he is within his rights as a small human to go to the bathroom if he goes straight back to bed.

One night, Bobby raced to the bathroom. There was a flush, running water, and the pitter patter of bare feet running back to bed. Normal. A little while later, he ran to the bathroom again. Flush. Water. Slam of his door as he went back to bed. Then a third time, near midnight, he ran to the toilet again. I got up, concerned that Bobby might have a stomach flu. I should have been glad to find a healthy boy staring up at me when I let myself into the bathroom. As it turns out, gladness was not the emotion that sprang forth.

Bobby's shirt was soaking wet, from collar to cuff. His feet were drenched, and the water had seeped up his pajama pants to his knees. When asked what he was doing, he gave a typical four-year-old reply. *Nuffin.*

I stepped forward to give the stern "Mom" glare more effectively, and my sock got wet. I looked down and discovered water sprawling from the toilet to the edge of the tub. Bobby's eyes followed mine, and he shrugged his shoulders when asked if he was playing in the bathtub.

I couldn't send the kid to bed in wet pajamas, although I'm sure Bobby wished I had once I followed wet footprints down the hall, entered his room, and found his bed soaked through. Blankets, sheets, pillows. All wet. I returned to the bathroom, fresh pajamas in hand. I inspected the bathroom, Sherlock Holmes style. Bathroom floor: Wet. Sink: Wet, but not overly so. The counter and the cabinet were both remarkably dry. Tub: Dry. I went deeper into the bathroom, a realization dawning. Toilet seat: Wet. Back of toilet: Wet. Exterior of toilet bowl: Dripping. My son. Was playing. In. The. TOILET.

Me: *Why were you playing in the toilet after bedtime?*
Bobby: *<Shrug>*
Me: *It's because it's fun, isn't it?*
Bobby: *<Worried look, then head shaking.> It isn't fun.*
Me: *I bet you're doing it because it's fun to sneak out of bed and play in the toilet.*
Bobby: *<Looks like maybe I'm on his side.> It's fun to play in the toilet. And it's not bad, I get to take a shower when you find me!*
Me: *It might be fun, but it's also yucky. There's germs that will make you sick, and look at the water all over the floor. I have to clean that up instead of going to bed. You and I could get sick from the toilet.*
Bobby: *<Realizes I'm not on his side.> But I get to take a shower.*
Me: *Yes. But this isn't going to be a fun shower. This is going to be a, "Get in. Get disinfected. Get out and go to bed," shower.*
Bobby: *Oh.*

If you're considering having kids someday, by all means, do. But keep in mind that you may find yourself standing over a sink in the middle of the night wringing what you hope is clean toilet water out of a stuffed animal. You've been warned.

SMALL BUSINESS OWNER

After several months of writing, housewifery, and moving my mom into our home to save her from an abusive relationship, I had a great idea. Around the time that I received the contract for *Age/Sex/Location: Love is just a click away*, Keith and I also started up a paintball customization company. He had been into the sport of paintball for many years at that point, and he was looking to start working on something he could enjoy more than being yelled at in his high-tech career.

The paintball business started gaining momentum around the same time that our neighbor was tapping on my home-office window. I told Keith I was considering renting office space a few miles away from the house, and he told me it was a ridiculous idea to rent and furnish an office for my writing just so I wouldn't have to keep telling the neighbor to leave me alone. Then, I tweaked the pitch. *But what if the office space was also a paintball store?* That did the trick and within a year we were renting a unit in an industrial park with a manufacturing shop and attached office.

We wanted to make sure that we did as much as we could to ensure the success of Gearheadz Paintball. Prior to renting the space, Keith and I invested into going to the Paintball Training Institute in Bluff City, Tennessee. The only formal school of paintball that I'm aware of, PTI provided us with hands-on learning that was invaluable when we opened our doors and started trying to convince local customers to give us money. We not only learned the mechanical workings of the leading products of the industry at that time, but PTI's instructors also provided us with a unique view of where paintball was going as an industry. Bob and Jeri, who ran the school, were happy to share their experiences as paintball entrepreneurs, and gave me room to go through final edits on my second novel between classes. Bob also wrote books, and we connected over the triumph and incredible anxiety that book making breeds.

The paintball startup was one of the most exciting projects that I've ever been a part of. Not only did I get to put all my previous store launch experience to use, but I also only had Keith and our friend and machinist, Ryan, to justify my actions to. The three of us slowly advanced our customization offerings, increased the amount of standard merchandise we carried to the point that the front office became a storefront, and once again I was working my butt off. The resulting strain and exhaustion was different from when I worked for the restaurant franchisees, though. Now, I was truly working for myself. I also had a troublesome new assistant. My son was born shortly after our front doors opened, and we ended up having to close up shop for a few weeks initially because of my medical complications.

Once I was stable, we plopped a playpen in the corner behind my desk, turned the sign to *Open*, and spent the next three years supporting our local paintball industry. We made some great friends in that time, who often made even better customers. I still feel incredibly blessed for all the hours we spent with our paintball buddies in the store. While we were building projects for, and selling products to these various customers, we were also given friendship by people with names like Uncle Biscuit, Deer Killer, El Fang, and Assma. That's the wonderful thing about a sport like paintball where players get to pick their own call-sign. People get creative.

Our shop was unique from our competitors at the time because selling product off the shelf wasn't our main focus. Sure, selling other companies' products was often the bulk of the store's income. But what Keith, Ryan, and I always focused on was customization for the individual. Within the limits of paintball's existing market, we were able to create some beautiful one-of-a-kind items. The feedback from players was slow growing, but when it finally came it was intense. We started to become fairly well-known in the United States and Canada. Our time in the limelight was a miniature brush with fame that was both awesome and incredibly odd to experience. None of us knew what to do when we got requests for autographs. The first time we got a request for an autographed product, Keith asked me who the customer wanted us to contact for a signature. It took us a minute to figure out that it was our scribbles that the fan wanted.

Despite Keith and Ryan's creativity, and our growing list of connections, Keith still had to maintain his day job as an engineer to cover our day to day expenses. We chose our shop's location partly because it was right across the street from the company he was working for. Five days a week, Keith would go to work, drop into the shop for lunch and to reply to emails, and go back to finish his shift. After work, he'd come back to the store and put in a few more hours until it was time to go home and put the baby to bed. We all worked the weekend for a while, but eventually Keith gave me the weekend off to have time to recover from a life of breastfeeding at the retail counter. For three years, Keith and I worked an unfathomable number of hours, six or seven days a week, and Ryan helped to pick up the slack when one or the other of us was too physically exhausted to keep going.

While Keith was playing professional across the street, I took the lulls between customers to write. Paintball was a boon to my writing portfolio and it wasn't long before I was submitting articles to industry magazines. I was picked up as a feature writer for *Paintball Chick*, a newspaper geared toward attracting more women into the sport. I started to do press releases for other paintball companies, wrote up product reviews and ad copy, and kept working on writing novels. The start of my science fiction series, *Adaline*, was written and published while I was sitting at the front desk of Gearheadz Paintball.

Through it all, the men's ability to innovate, and our ability to swallow our pride and ask for help from others, put us in position to work with some of the longest lasting anchors in paintball history. We were given the opportunity to acquire or enhance other brands and develop products with the help of other businesses. The support that we received from what outsiders would have dubbed our "competitors," was empowering and emotional. When longtime players state that they stick with paintball because of the community, they aren't just blowing smoke. Although there's a lot of drama in a market made up of so many microentrepreneurs, the general level of support and kindness that perseveres is unmatched in the business world.

Our rise through paintball was swift. It was one of the most exciting times in my life, and I wish that it could have continued. But 2013 would change all of that. In paintball, a couple of mega conglomerates started a race to buy out and absorb or bury the best manufacturers in the industry. In case you're wondering, monopolies are never a good thing. Outside of the office, that year was the beginning of tragedy for Keith and me personally. It was a year that our business, some of our closest friendships, and much of our family wouldn't survive.

Before the paintball store opened, we ran Gearheadz Paintball from our house. Keith's workshop for creating custom products was an eight by ten foot shed at the head of our driveway. We converted a spare bedroom in the house into a warehouse by installing rows of wire shelves. The stock didn't stay contained for long though, and soon bins of paintball gear were overflowing into other areas of the house. I did all our marketing and accounting from our home office, and part of why I ended up pushing to rent a space was because what had once been a spacious suburban home had become a paintball stockpile that we happened to sleep in.

One of the biggest challenges of working the business from home, aside from having to move stacks of paint pods before I could print an invoice, was that many of the manufacturers wouldn't release product to us if we didn't have a brick and mortar store. The theory behind the practice of excluding web-only sales was that it would support those people who were invested in paying rent on a storefront each month. The reality though was that being excluded from whole catalogues of goods was a huge hurdle to overcome as we built our business.

I persevered through all the denials for business accounts, and eventually I stumbled into Ninja Paintball's wholesale call listing. Ninja was the leader in paintball high pressure air devices, and I wasn't feeling very positive about what the result of my calling them would be. Imagine my surprise when I was directed to one of their business account guys, Rob.

Rob: *So, I've been told that you'd like to set up a new account. Can you give me your business name?*

Me: *Gearheadz Paintball, LLC.*

Rob: *What? You're… Wait.*

Me: *Gearheadz Paintball, LLC. G-e-a-r-h-e-a-d-z….*

Rob: *No, I mean, wait. Hang on.*

<dead air>

Rob: *You guys made the Stormin' Norman?*

Me: *Yeah, we sure did.*

Rob: *I'm looking at you right now! You're in Action Pursuit Games!*

Me: *Oh, yeah. We entered one of their build contests and they chose us as one of the winners for this month's magazine.*

Rob: *I can't believe I'm talking to you right now. This is so cool!*

Rob was our first excited fan, and gave us our very first business-to-business dealer account. If it wasn't for his enthusiasm, and willingness to trust that we were working toward something great, we may never have gotten Gearheadz Paintball out of our living room and into a building all its own.

Whenever we hit a roadblock in our march toward success, or we hit a slump that made us question whether we were doing the right thing, someone like Rob would inevitably pop up and tell us how excited they were to be talking to us. We built a following that helped to keep our passion for paintball alive, and boosted our confidence when we needed a pick-me-up. Rob, and everyone like him, became the true cornerstone of our business. Without their enthusiasm, the whole operation would have fallen apart.

MOURNER

The afternoon of August 20, 2013, I had been getting text messages from my bestie, Beth. I was in the middle of something, or the baby was causing me grief, or the store had customers. I don't remember. But I replied that I was busy and would have to catch up with her some other time. I had no idea that I'd never talk to Beth again. Hours later, a young man with a horrendous driving record sped through a stop sign and t-boned Beth's car. The impact took Beth's life. She and her daughter were on their way home following her daughter's weekly visit with her dad, and the horrific accident severely injured the little girl. We thought we might lose her, too.

When I got the message from a mutual friend about the accident, I was devastated. I had lost one of my life's anchors. Never one to maintain long-term ties with people, my friendship with Beth had been my longest relationship. We'd met in a chatroom online in 2002, and although thousands of miles usually separated us, she was always present in my computer, through the mail, and on my phone. I followed her case, in which the offending driver was not charged with anything more severe than failure to stop at a stop sign. The anger and sadness that I felt following those events was more than I thought I could bear.

Still, somehow, I managed to pull myself together enough to continue lugging the baby to work with me, and Keith and I kept on building Gearheadz Paintball. There was another lapse in productivity in January of 2014 though when my mom called to tell me that my paternal grandfather had passed away. His story was less horrific; he passed away peacefully while waiting for some dessert to be delivered to him in his recliner. I brushed that loss aside as best I could. Functionally, nothing changed for me. As may have been noted throughout the reading of this story, I severed most contact with my father as a young person. I won't derail the momentum of your reading here with that laundry list of reasons, other than to say that there are sometimes things done, or not done; things said, or not said, that cause you to not talk to a person for decades at a time.

The real issue with cutting ties with my father is that I have a real hang-up with making sure that I'm seen as being fair, and for many years I didn't think it would be fair for me to keep my grandparents in my social loop while ignoring their son. So, at the time of my grandfather's death, I could compartmentalize the event since I hadn't seen or spoken with him in several years. Emotionally, it was a heavier loss than I let on, though, and it made me reevaluate my definition of "fairness" where my familial relationships were concerned.

As I was pondering whether or not to reconnect with my grandmother in light of her husband's death, my dog did some weird acrobatic something-or-other while we were at work just before Valentine's Day. We came home to find he'd injured his spine in six places and made the difficult decision to put him down. It truly was a difficult choice as he'd been my shadow for nine years at that point. On the day that we were going to take him to the vet to be euthanized, I took him to work with me one last time. He'd been our shop dog since the beginning of Gearheadz Paintball and I wanted him to sleep on his bed in the store one more day. We didn't make it through the whole shift though. That day, February 11th, Keith's sister called me in hysterics. Their mom had died suddenly and without warning.

That day was truly one of the worst days in my life. I couldn't get in touch with Keith on his cell phone, and when I called the front desk of the huge corporation he worked for, they weren't able to locate him in the building. I couldn't just wait for him to turn up at the shop after work. His family needed us. So, I shut the store down with a note on the window, loaded my toddler and all his mobile baby-gear in the car, carried my injured dog (I forgot to mention he was a Boxer/Great Dane cross and did not fit in a purse) to the car and set him up with as comfortable a bed in the back of the hatchback as I could. I raced across the street, phone to my ear, calling my husband on redial until he answered. By then he was back in an area where he had phone signal and he staggered out of the building once he comprehended that his mom was gone.

We raced as gingerly as we could an hour and a half north to Longview, Washington where Keith's family were gathering. Cognizant of my dog, twitching in pain with every turn of the wheel or bump in the road, the trip was a blur of fighting the urges to both drive like every second counted, and to keep Goliath comfortable. Once we arrived, it was clear that the trip had not done my poor dog any favors. We got everyone settled as best we could. The next morning, we drove Goliath to a vet nearby and had him put to sleep.

Following the funeral service for Debbie, Keith's mom, my dedication to our store pushed us back home. Just weeks later, my maternal great-grandfather passed away. Chet was in his nineties and his health had declined steadily in his late years, so his passing wasn't a shocking surprise. But at that point, all the death was becoming too much to bear. Keith talked about closing Gearheadz Paintball down, and I insisted that we keep it going. I was sure life was going to settle out and I didn't want either of us to regret making such a major decision during all our grief.

The paintball store kept crawling down the notch of importance though when Keith's maternal grandfather also passed away. We put paintball on hold again and returned to Longview to support the family. Al was also an elderly gentleman, but his passing just weeks after Debbie was hard for everyone to take. I know that sometimes when family members pass away so close together, there's a sense of relief that neither member is passing into the great unknown alone. Maybe other family members felt that way, but for me it just created more anger and resentment.

Throughout our attempt at returning to a normal life despite the insanity stacking up within us, we discovered that Goliath's cat had lost his mind. Goliath was not only a large dog, but he also had some liberties that most other dogs don't enjoy. Getting to have his own cat was one of them. His little buddy, Dummy, was an aptly named ridiculous animal. But when Dummy arrived at our home years earlier, he bonded to Goliath something fierce. The cat seemed like it had lost its soul after Goliath was gone. Dummy patrolled the neighborhood, crying and yowling for Goliath for weeks. It was obvious that he was looking for his lost friend. Dummy was run over by a car during his search.

The summer was mostly uneventful mortality-wise, and so we did our best to plaster smiles on our faces and return to work. There was so much loss to process, that Keith and I felt numb to all of it. The numbness is probably the only thing that allowed us to keep moving forward with our day-to-day tasks and responsibilities. Despite us needing to be closed for several weeks because of grief, services, and travel, our shop seemed to rally that summer. We had a lot of ground to catch up on regarding our sales figures. Being closed all that time, we still had to pay our rent and utilities on the shop, not to mention we'd bought a bunch of inventory that was just lying around with no one to push it onto customers with open wallets. Ryan did a fantastic job of filling in the gaps, but one person can't do the work of three for an extended period. We kept our external cool though, and many people had no idea of the turmoil boiling just below the surface.

September brought news of another death in my familial loop. Jeanie, a woman who'd been friends with my mom since I was a child succumbed to cancer. There were so many odds stacked against her, and both myself and my mother had wished that we'd known more about her battle with the disease so that we could have offered more support. But as a caretaker herself, Jeanie probably hadn't wanted to bother us with more sadness. Ultimately, my mom suffered greatly following the loss of one of her closest friends.

By the end of 2014, we were a wreck. The pain in our hearts was heavy, and we looked again at the paintball store. We loved Gearheadz Paintball. It was a monster all its own that had spawned fans, community, friendships, and connections that we never dreamed we'd ever have. But at the end of that year, we were so battered and bruised emotionally that we knew we needed to let it go. Keith and I were still putting in fifty to a hundred hours a week depending on what events were going on in the area, and special projects being produced. Our toddler had never known life without a full-time job (plus overtime) and now that he was talking and learning to read I realized that I needed to move him into an environment where he could be paid attention to. We made one of the toughest calls in our marriage, and decided that 2015 would be the year we closed the storefront.

The beginning of 2015 also brought another passing. My great-grandmother, Lola, passed away a year to the day of her husband. Her time of death was within an hour of Chet's time of passing, a testament to the bond of love that held those two old birds together. It was a bond not shared by their respective children, however, and the trauma of their combined losses was compounded as familial drama unfolded and inheritances, property, and trusts were grabbed at and disputed in that year between their deaths.

As we began to empty out the store, running sales, and counting down the days to the end of our lease, 2015 also claimed my great-uncle Fred. He was an interesting man who was full of stories, which slowly dwindled as they were wiped over by a progression of dementia. Although otherwise healthy at his annual physical just months prior, he suddenly fell ill with leukemia and passed away from complications when a bout of pneumonia took hold. The well of grief had gone dry by this point, and although I did, and do, feel sad for his loss I wasn't able to cry for his absence the way he deserved.

Years later, I still don't understand why or how we lost so much of our family support network so quickly. Looking at the losses from a theological standpoint, I have yet to find the purpose that a higher power would have for inflicting so much pain onto one family. Physiologically, I am both thankful for and wary of the way our bodies kept moving forward through the grief. It truly is amazing what a being can persevere through, and often outsiders don't have any way of gleaning how horrific someone's life can be as they smile and continue to serve others. Psychologically, I'm still dealing with the grief that came from the rapid-fire dispatch of so many people who loved, inspired, and supported me.

The only thing that I can glean from this time of sorrow is that we truly discovered who we could count on when things were a wreck. Support faltered from many we expected it from, and arrived from places we'd never imagined. Each time Death knocked on our door, our priorities shifted a little and the list of people who we were willing to allow to hold us back became shorter. Ultimately, losing so much opened our eyes to what we were doing to ourselves as we tried to live with one foot in the American Dream, and the other foot in the false security of corporate life. Letting go of the paintball store was certainly a step back from one of Keith's greatest passions, but it allowed me to have time to explore my rebirth of interest in agriculture, simple living, and of course gave me more time to write.

Ultimately, letting go of paintball would lead to letting go of the high-pressure, high-tech job Keith was toiling away at also. More on that later.

The two weeks between Keith's mom, Debra's, passing and her funeral were both the worst, and the most comforting weeks we've had as a family. Most of our waking hours were spent cleaning Debra and Steve's house, preparing for family to visit, and hunting for treasures that Deb had stashed away over the years. It was a macabre scavenger hunt, but each closet and dresser drawer revealed new secrets that brought to light layers of Deb's history and personality that I'd never known before.

Although there were a wide variety of trinkets, long forgotten wardrobes, and vintage dishes to find, there was a buzz of excitement around the house as we each began to find money tucked away in tins and long-forgotten pockets. There were gift cards in the dining room. Cash in the bedrooms. Rolled up bills and coins found in coats and disused purses.

Among the jewelry found under dressers, presents (some wrapped, some not) tucked in the backs of closets, and bath towels in every shade of purple and green, the family found enough cash to pay for Deb's funeral service. In life, she'd been the woman who had three of everything, and was willing to share her bounty with others. It didn't take long to discover that after her passing, she was still taking care of us. Everyone had a birthday or Christmas present to open. We were all thankful for her ability to squirrel away everything we needed, even if it was years before we needed it.

DISSOLUSIONIST

By spring of 2015, Keith had convinced me that it was time to close our business. The truth was, he'd never wavered from his decision that he was ready to shut Gearheadz Paintball down weeks after his mom's passing in 2014. I'd convinced myself his desire to walk away from the shop was a knee-jerk reaction to grief. I finally understood a year later that he'd reached some clarity on how much of life we were missing out on by pushing ourselves to be successful entrepreneurs.

Our lease was ending in June, and rather than do the song and dance of negotiating a new rental agreement with the business park, we notified them that we were moving. Okay, so I still wasn't on board with completely shutting things down. But I agreed that downsizing our work, taking things back to the house, and only taking on one project at a time was something worth doing.

We didn't tell many people that we were going to close the brick and mortar store. Our business partner and investors knew, but no one visiting the store knew anything was amiss until we stopped making inventory orders in the spring and the shelves started to go bare. We didn't worry about landing any giant consignment sales deals with our suppliers when we headed to our spring events and instead focused on selling out of as much product as possible. Our goal was to pay off the few debts we had as a company before we returned our operations to the home office. It was at SuperGame, our local industry's largest trade show and scenario game, that we finally announced we were closing.

Through paintball we have met some wonderful people. We made friends with quite a few of our customers and some of those relationships persist today. The announcement that we were closing was followed by a lot of supportive hugs, many shrugs of understanding, and then a lot of dead air. Things were lonely for a while as people simply didn't know what to do to support us. After all the deaths in our family, extended periods of having to close the shop due to depression and grief, the flop of a couple of our final projects while tensions were high in the machine shop... I think even our closest friends were at a loss for the right thing to say or do. The phone stopped ringing, Facebook stopped dinging, and I caught up with every email in my inbox for the first time.

The plus side of the awkward silence was that Keith and I got a lot of work done. We sold most of our fixtures on Craigslist, packed up the remaining inventory and tooling, and put it in a cheap storage unit to be dealt with later. We flipped the store's sign to Closed and reclassified ourselves as a home-based business. Then we took a deep breath and realized that life as we'd known it was over. Weeks after moving Gearheadz Paintball back home, life shifted again. If we'd renewed our lease and kept fighting to keep our shop alive, it would have destroyed us. But because we'd decided to turn the battle into a part-time endeavor, we just happened to have the time and finances for the immense challenges that would arrive next.

Of all the casualties that arrived after the close of our company's brick and mortar presence, the one that impacted us the most was the dissolution of Keith's closest friendship. In our company's growth, he had brought in a friend to work as our machinist and through pure quantity of hours spent together their friendship grew until I began to refer to Ryan as Keith's "other wife."

There is a well-known and long-standing piece of business advice that you should never work with friends. It is one that is often ignored by highly intelligent people who want to surround themselves with love and talent, and despite my early reservations, it's a piece of wisdom that we chose to ignore. The fact is, working with friends is a lot of fun when things are going well. We celebrated a lot of successes together, and when we were all in the groove we produced some truly amazing pieces of art.

Unfortunately, friendships are strained when business isn't going so well. Ryan did his best to keep our doors open in our absence. He was there as he was able during our trips to see family and attend funerals during our rapid-fire losses. But as our struggles became deeper, I imagine the pressure to be available wore him thin.

We had a lot of plans and opportunities in place for things to be more profitable for everyone, but for reasons I won't go into here, much of our intended growth for Ryan and his pocketbook didn't meet any of our expectations. In the end, a regular job with a standard paycheck became the answer for Ryan and when we moved the machining side of the business to his garage, he ultimately decided to move on to greener pastures.

Keith and Ryan's marriage dissolved over the course of one last complicated custom order. It was a breakup that would have hit the tabloids if we were more famous. The fallout was deep enough that Keith ended up cancelling the custom contract, something we'd never done in all our years as a business. As business people, it became clear that we were no longer able to foster either our friendship or our business in a way that was healthy or sane. We lost both in the end.

Years later, I still wish Ryan and his family the best. Through Facebook stalking it appears that life has continued in positive directions for them, and I'm glad that he has been able to stay active in the paintball community that gave all of us so much. We hope to get back out there ourselves one day and see how things go when the paint flies.

CAREGIVER (PART DEUX)

Weeks after we closed the doors to the Gearheadz Paintball storefront for the last time, amid trying to get through one last custom project and the frustration of a battle of wills with Ryan, Keith got sick.

Initially, in June of 2015, we thought he had a rough bout of food poisoning. It seemed like he ate a bad meal while we were on a camping trip with family. Although no one else got sick, he was miserable and spent most of the weekend curled up in a ball in our sleeping bags. By the end of summer, Keith was having illness related to food with some frequency. It took a while, but eventually a trip to the doctor was made.

Okay folks, now we're going to get intimate. I'm going to pass my author voice over to the melodic stylings of Mr. Barry White. Turn those lights down low, turn on some slow jams and get comfy. Here we go.

Keith was having some rectal bleeding. *Awwww, yeah.* Then he eased into some colon spasms. *Oooooooh.* He had a rectal exam that ended with a referral for two colonoscopies. *That's it, girl (eyebrow wiggle).* Got nice and close to a gastroenterologist with some wicked sexy cameras that went straight up the butt. *Ooooh! You know what I like.*

Thanks, Barry. I'm going to take the reins back. That was a lot less sexy than I imagined it being when I was half asleep, thinking about a non-disgusting way to describe what has become a life filled with various stages of angry poop. There's just no pretty way to put it. Life turned to shit.

Initially, Keith was diagnosed with severe hemorrhoids. Being a desk jockey engineer who came to his second job (Gearheadz) to sit at a workbench and write quotes for service, then went home to sit on the couch to play video games to decompress wasn't doing his butt region any favors. But even after we made changes to help repair his derriere, something was still going on internally so more tests were done. After a round of bloodwork and the first colonoscopy, Keith was diagnosed with Crohn's disease.

If you aren't familiar with Crohn's, as I wasn't, here are the cliff notes. Crohn's is a disease that affects the digestive tract. It can attack anywhere in the tract, from your esophagus to your anus, but our experience primarily involved an inflamed colon. What happens is a section of your digestive tract becomes chronically inflamed and then stops functioning. This is a real problem for anyone who likes to eat, digest, and poop normally.

After the Crohn's diagnosis, Keith began a series of treatments to help his colon to reduce its inflammation. This caused some issues. Since we'd been relatively healthy before this bout with Keith's butt, we'd chosen a high deductible plan for our insurance policy to save money on monthly premiums. The result was that we spent the fall months of 2015 shelling out our first five thousand dollars in treatments. Any relief we might have had once our deductible was met was squashed once we discovered that most of the medications Keith was prescribed weren't covered by our insurance at all (because guess what, they're fucking expensive) so every trip to the pharmacy turned into hundreds and sometimes thousands of dollars passed across the counter in exchange for pharmaceutical drugs. None of the treatments worked, and in fact, the primary medications he was taking seemed to be making Keith worse. By early winter he was spending several days a week in bed, drenched in sweat and holding his guts gingerly while they spasmed for hours.

We were exceedingly lucky during Keith's spiral that we had already closed the storefront. Not only did I have time available to then become a full-time caregiver, but money we'd previously been investing in our businesses expansion was now available for medical treatment. Keith's day job also afforded him a lot of vacation time, a several-week sabbatical because of his seniority, and finally some comprehensive medical leave so that he could take several months off work while he grappled with food, standing upright, and spending several hours each day on the toilet.

When the gastroenterologist's treatments weren't working, we went back several times to tell him so. Keith's body was spasming so furiously that he was pooping out most of the medications wholly intact. He was literally flushing money down the toilet every time he went to the bathroom. The doctor put him on a series of restrictive diets (he spent that Thanksgiving eating nothing but bananas, dry toast, plain white rice, and applesauce) and doubled the dosages on the meds. When we voiced our concerns that we didn't think this course of treatment was working, he belittled us and convinced us he was the professional and we should just follow his directions.

Our complacency with the gastroenterologist didn't last long. It became immediately apparent that doubling down on these giant pills wasn't getting Keith anywhere. We asserted ourselves with the doctor and he green-lit a second colonoscopy to see if the inflammation had spread. The colonoscopy prep was torture for Keith, and he had a horrible time getting "cleaned out" enough for the procedure. His body kept ejecting rectal bile until the absolute last second, and despite concerns from the hospital nursing staff, the colonoscopy went ahead as planned.

I was waiting in the hall when the doctor emerged.

Good news. Everything looks normal. The colon inflammation is gone. It isn't Crohn's after all.

I stared at the doctor, flabbergasted. So then, what was so wrong?

Nothing. There aren't any abnormalities. Your husband's issues are cured. Why don't you look happy?

I was glad that it wasn't Crohn's, sure. Crohn's is a horrible disease and no one should ever hope to have it. But something was wrong. Keith couldn't keep food in his system. He'd lost seventy pounds in just a few months. He couldn't sit at a desk to work, and couldn't work from the toilet in his office. He couldn't even stop pooping long enough to make the fifteen-minute commute from our home toilet to his office toilet if he'd wanted to try. He'd been on five restrictive diets to cancel out food allergies and sensitivities. His body had stopped processing any kind of fiber and was ejecting anything stronger than non-pulp juice.

The doctor shook his head. *I'll review the video again at the office, but from where I stand now, I don't see anything wrong with him.*

At our follow-up appointment, the doctor confirmed Keith was cured. Keith asked for more paperwork to be filed to extend his leave at work while we tried to figure out what else could be causing these horrific symptoms. The doctor looked stunned. *You're missing work?* We had both told the gastroenterologist and his staff that Keith had transitioned from working at the office to trying to work at home, and that it failed because he couldn't be logged in long enough to get anything done. This same doctor had helped us file the paperwork for medical leave based on the Crohn's diagnosis weeks before. It was blatantly obvious that he truly hadn't been paying attention to anything beyond his script pad. We fired him.

Then, we panicked. A person can't be on extended medical leave without a diagnosis, or a medical professional who will document that they're trying to find out what a diagnosis might be. Keith went back to our general practitioner and explained all that had happened since the initial referral to the gastro. We'd been with Dr. Nguyen, our general doc, for many years. He has always been patient and attentive, and in this very delicate situation his ability to listen and work with his patients was a godsend. He took over Keith's care while we searched for another gastroenterologist, and helped us to prove to Keith's employer and their insurance company that he needed to continue his leave from work while we tried to sort out what the hell was wreaking havoc on his body.

Enter medical marijuana. One of the major problems that Keith was experiencing was a severe spasm of his digestive tract whenever food was introduced. We'd done all kinds of research into alternative diets, treatments, voodoo magic, and toilet worship during our education about Crohn's and one thing that came up repeatedly was the use of cannabis to slow the digestive tract down, relieve pain and pressure without pharmaceuticals (which are all hard on your gut, even as they are supposed to be repairing it), and assist with a general feeling of wellbeing. We'd tried everything else, and since marijuana was legal in Oregon, Keith started doing hands-on research of the strains available in our area.

I won't go on a soapbox diatribe about my feelings on cannabis other than to say it's the first treatment Keith tried that allowed him to begin to eat consistently. The downside was that he had to medicate continually, and so there were chunks of the day where he'd disappear into the bathroom or the privacy of our back yard to medicate. As soon as the effects wore off, the spasms and pain returned. But the quickness of the relief that smoking marijuana presented was striking, and the results were such a relief to us. For the first time in months, I had a husband who I could hang out with again, my son had a dad he could play videogames with again, and we were able to look toward the future and talk about what would come next.

The biggest drawback to medical marijuana use was that even though its use was legal, it wasn't approved by Keith's employer. He could have been popping a Percocet at his desk and it would have been fine and dandy. But there's no way that most corporate offices will let you go outside and inhale your medication, and Keith's employer was no exception. This presented a very real problem for us. Now we had a solution for the biggest problem in Keith's life, being able to eat, but for him to get back to a state where he could return to work he'd have to continue pursuing western medicine for an official diagnosis and a treatment that could work non-stop for ten hours a day. We both discussed the idea of him going back to his engineering job and sneaking pot into breaks between meetings, but that wasn't realistic. For one, as soon as his on-campus medicating was found out, he'd be fired. Second, the medical marijuana didn't cure him. He still couldn't take extended trips away from the toilet, still could barely go to the store across the street because the gut pain made it difficult to walk, and was only somewhat functional for four or five hours out of the day. But the tiny bit of relief Keith was feeling made me hopeful that we were heading in a direction that would one day allow him to return to his career.

The second gastroenterologist we got a referral to was wonderful. A sprite of a woman, she seemed to sprinkle fairy dust on your poop story to help make you and your family feel better. She reviewed Keith's medical files from the previous gastro and confirmed to us that Keith didn't have Crohn's. She empathized with the journey we'd been on, and diagnosed Keith with stress-induced irritable bowel syndrome (IBS). The diagnosis presented a whole new host of problems. Keith was referred to a nutritionist who offered a new restrictive diet (which was laughable at that point because his diet basically consisted of plain chicken and noodles at the time). The new gastro also encouraged Keith to use a pharmaceutical antispasmodic which helped increase the spectrum of what he could eat.

She did note that we both seemed depressed, and encouraged Keith to talk to someone about the emotional side of what was happening. His mental recovery isn't my story to tell so I won't go into specifics about how he was feeling (although if you put yourself in his shoes I'm sure you can figure out that he wasn't overly cheerful). From my perspective, it was a relief to have someone else willing to listen to our story who believed in the severity of the symptoms and could understand that Keith's day-to-day life, and our ability to function as a family were both being impacted.

Medication continued, symptoms persisted, and we began to understand that there's no hard and fast treatment for IBS. We all did our best to relieve Keith's stress as a means to curing is symptoms, but nothing seemed to work. I began having panic attacks at the grocery store as I looked at all the food that was available for purchase, but that might put Keith into a bedridden flare of symptoms. We started looking at how long it was taking for improvements to Keith's gut to come about compared to the amount of medical leave Keith had left. The whole poopy mess ended with a trip to the emergency room that resulted in many months of outpatient treatment.

As a caretaker, wife, and partner, I was desperate for something to work. I researched healing foods in the middle of the night. I packed the car with activities and snacks for our toddler while we carted Daddy to his various appointments. My days of caretaking were interrupted by stacks of medical paperwork, insurance disputes and appeals, coordinating between multiple doctors' offices, and shopping pharmacies and medical marijuana dispensaries for the medicines Keith needed at prices we might be able to afford.

When winter turned to spring, and spring started looking like summer, it became clear. Keith couldn't return to his career. We couldn't afford our mortgage payment without the Silicone Forest job, and it was time to make another change.

Although my life was in shambles, closing our business breathed new life into my writing. I was puttering along with an idea for the second book in the *Adaline* series, but I was having a horrible time putting it down on paper. During our downward spiral in real life, I began escaping into the horrifically delightful world of author Chelsea Cain and her femme fatale, fictional serial killer Gretchen Lowell. I also got run down by zombies in the wee hours of sleeplessness as I sped through the pages of Sarah Lyons Fleming's Until the End of the World series. As a result of these ladies' influences, and a long-standing fascination with the psychopathy of serial murderers, I decided to try my hand at writing a book where not everyone survived.

Although my first novel, *Age/Sex/Location: Love is just a click away*, was a contemporary romance, I'd become most widely known for my science fiction novel, *Adaline*. My second full-length book, *Adaline* is a clean read appropriate for all ages, and I've had multiple fans tell me that they enjoyed reading it with their kids. Sure, it has mad scientists, robot overlords, and a creepy sterility that keeps an entire race of clones in check, but *Adaline* is a young man's thinking book in the end. The kids think it's awesome to have a world without parents (until they realize how crappy robots are at caretaking), and the adults understand the undercurrent of political rally to blend us all into one cohesive hipster without opinion or desire for forward motion.

So, when the idea for *S is for Serial* came to me, I decided I couldn't just throw my standard pseudonym, Denise Kawaii, on it. I decided to call my author alter-ego D.K. Greene. D.K. stands for Denise Kawaii, and Greene was spawned from my odd fascination with Gary Ridgeway. Ridgeway is commonly known as the Green River Killer and was arrested in the general area of my stomping grounds in 2001 while I was trying to be a permanent resident of

Seattle. I followed the lead up to his trial intently upon my move to Hawaii shortly thereafter.

What I discovered while writing about crazy people, long-dead victims, and an extreme case of daddy issues, was that writing a book about people with worse issues than I have is both cathartic and fun. *S is for Serial* is the fastest book I've penned to date. The first manuscript took about seven weeks to write, and I had a heck of a good time road tripping around the Pacific Northwest in search of places where a killer might dump a body and integrating those locations into my story. The editing took several months as the topic was unsettling to Keith (my primary editor at the time), and I had to rewrite sections to make certain characters appear less familiar to friends and former coworkers who might later read the book. I didn't want any former peers to pick up a copy and realize that I fantasized about burying them deep in the woods.

Keith was so ill in November of 2015 that when *S is for Serial* was first published he spent the entire release party in bed, avoiding looking at the food and drinks that were spread out for guests. It wasn't until the day of the party that I realized my entire food spread was made up of thing that were off his restrictive diet. I was so upset at his illness and my lack of foresight (why wouldn't someone on a water and bread diet want to be around a wine and cheese party?) that I almost cancelled the party at the last second. At the encouragement of my sister-in-law, Alison, I sucked it up and welcomed a house full of readers. That was my most successful release of a book in the end, and I sold out of my first printing within the first couple of weeks of release.

S is for Serial was a good reminder that even when shit hits the fan, positive life can happen. Somehow, I found the inspiration and drive to write a novel, launch a secondary author pseudonym, and promote them both well enough to be as widely distributed in a few weeks as *Adaline* had been in the two previous years. I'm glad that *S is for Serial* leapt out of me so easily as it was a welcome distraction from the writer's block I was experiencing with *Biocide,* the eventual sequel to *Adaline.*

Sometimes, you just have to travel where your imagination leads you, even if it means taking out your frustrations on the hapless residents of a fictional killer's fantasy.

ESTATE LIQUIDATOR

We made the decision to sell our house in 2016 before we couldn't afford it. The decision didn't sneak up on us. In truth, we had spent a couple of years casually downsizing our belongings and planning on building a tiny house to live in. Even in the thick of our success in paintball, we knew that we wanted to reduce our lifestyle to a more manageable pace. We'd known for years that the level of stress and activity we were subject to daily was unsustainable, and so we'd been on the path of getting out of our house long before Keith's illness arrived on our doorstep.

What had once been a process that was tiptoed through with dreamy eyes and lofty aspirations suddenly became imminent reality. We had to sell most of what we owned, get the property cleaned up and get it listed before we ran out of money for mortgage payments.

The market was right, with Keith's medical leave coming to an end we knew we had a finite amount of income we could count on, and once the career was gone there would be nothing holding us to the town we lived in.

… you know, aside from the blood, sweat, and tears we'd spent over the previous decade making that house our home. But who has time to think about that when buried in crisis?

Keith wanted to help, and lord knows he tried, but he was shackled to the bed or the toilet most of the time. That left the bulk of the heavy lifting to me, and I busied my time posting ads on Craigslist, listing things on eBay, and coordinating a series of garage sales to get rid of anything that we thought we could live without. A lifetime of collectibles, furniture, cookie cutters, and Tupperware left the house one box at a time. Toward the end, it was leaving the house a Suburban load at a time as we ran out of things of value and just needed to get stuff out of the building. I'm sure the kind folks at Goodwill appreciated all that vintage dinnerware and the truck load of floor lamps.

I was blessed in that my mom was doing well mentally in those days, and she made herself available for cleaning up the landscaping, painting bedrooms, shuffling boxes around otherwise empty rooms, and watching Bobby so I could take a nap or a shower from time to time. Keith's dad put a lot of effort into our move from the house as well. He brought down a sprayer and painted the entire exterior of the house in a weekend. It was a bright blue that I'd wanted our home to be for years, and we added a white trim. Just as we were exiting the property, all the projects on the list of "to-dos" that had been hanging on the side of the refrigerator got done. It looked like the house I'd always wanted it to be, although the emptier it got the less it felt like our home.

Our parents' rally to help, and the help of many other friends and family who volunteered, was truly the only thing that kept us from just setting the whole building on fire and hoping that no one would ask any questions. We had friends who brought us carefully cooked meals or provided us with a narrow selection of meats and grains that Keith could digest. We had others who hung out with me while I waited to pick Keith up or drop him off for his next round of doctors' appointments. Family arrived with trucks and power tools to remove debris from our property and disassemble a hot tub that we'd been trying unsuccessfully to get rid of for years. To everyone who was a part of our lives during the preparation of putting the house up for sale, I offer my deepest gratitude. We were so physically exhausted and emotionally scattered then that I can't even remember all the efforts made to help us through, but I know they were done and life would have been harder without so many helping hands.

The effort put in by everyone was worthwhile. In one of our few strokes of luck during that time of our lives, the housing market was in a perfect place for us to make a grand escape. There was a short supply of homes and a huge demand to buy. We had an offer within two days, accepted it, and started the final stages of moving back into Keith's childhood home.

When we bought our house, we had no idea how long we'd be living there. Our plan was to be there three or four years, then keep the house as a rental when we upgraded to a farm on the outskirts of town. Land ownership has been a common goal for Keith and me since the beginning, and we believed when we purchased our house that it was merely a stepping stone to our "real" house. Little did we know that we'd be in that home for many years, that it would see the rise and fall of our business, the writing of several novels, the birth of our son, and the comings and goings of many cats and a couple of dogs.

Since we intended to rent to families or college students, we purchased a home with more rooms than we needed. Immediately after we moved in, we rented out one of the rooms to help cover a portion of the mortgage. We used a second spare bedroom as a guest room, an emergency shelter for family in need, a warehouse, and finally, a nursery. When we found out there was a baby coming, I decided the room needed to be updated. Many people don't know this about me, but in addition to writing I like to pretend to be a painter. One of my favorite things to paint are murals.

I was near the end of my pregnancy in 2012 when we moved Gearheadz Paintball from our house into the store, so at eight or nine months in I started sketching a mural on the wall. My mom had helped me make some custom bedding for the crib, and one of the sets we made had an awesome dragon quilt. Inspired, I started painting a giant dragon sitting on a hill, leaning down over a prince.

The prince leaned up high and reached for a hug. A heart hung between them.

I wouldn't finish the mural until several weeks after our son was born, but it did get completed and was more beautiful than I'd hoped it would be. The mural became my favorite thing about our house, and when we discussed putting the house on the market I became heartbroken over the idea of painting over it to make the home more show ready. Luckily, the way the market was, our agent told us we could leave it. Keith knew I didn't want to get rid of the mural, and that I didn't need another project on my plate anyway. So, we left it.

There was no mention of the mural during the sale negotiation, and I was relieved when painting over it wasn't a part of the list of repairs and cosmetic changes requested. Several weeks after we moved out and the ownership passed on to the buyer, I drove through the neighborhood. There were toys in the driveway, and the curtains were drawn as I crept by. The dragon peeked out through the window, and I smiled when the prince reached up to try for another hug.

TAXI DRIVER

After we sold the house, we moved across state lines. The hour and a half trek north brought us into the center of Keith's childhood world. Our son took ownership of Keith's old bedroom, and we moved our belongings into Keith's late mother's room. The three of us began using the bathroom where his mom had suffered her fatal heart attack. The whole living situation was a shock to our emotions in ways we hadn't anticipated. But I didn't have time to deal with that.

Although we'd made a sizeable move, it had taken us so long to find a group of doctors that could work together to help Keith navigate his health that we continued driving him back to Portland,

Oregon for his ongoing medical care. This was a great idea overall, though it meant we spent between two and four days a week in the car, shuttling back and forth between our new home in Washington to his doctors in Oregon for tests, treatments, and general puzzle solving. We were spending between six and eight hours each trip on the road, sitting in office lobbies and waiting for the next appointment to start.

The constant travel was harder on me than it was on Keith. For the first time in his life he discovered that he could sleep in the car, so most trips he curled up under a quilt, smothered his head in a pillow and shut his eyes on the world. That left me to entertain myself while trying to stay awake and not fall prey to highway hypnosis.

From June to December of 2016 we made the trek back and forth. Because we were in constant motion, I began to feel like I didn't live anywhere anymore. I slept in one state but still lived a good portion of my life in another. Although we were in Portland sometimes several times a week, we didn't have enough time or energy to see any of our friends or family there, aside from the odd thirty-minute lunch or dinner before we hit the road again. The task of getting from here to there and back again became a very lonely business.

As always though, I used my odd chunks of time wisely. I took my laptop with me, fully charged, nearly everywhere we went. I'd write as I waited for Keith to return from appointments. If I wasn't feeling writerly, I'd bring a book or two with me to read instead. I can't count how many hours I read and wrote in the backseat that year. It was enough for me to write most of *Biocide*. There was also time for me to read nearly three dozen books, catch up with phone calls and emails to friends, and follow through with a stress relief program that was provided for me by our insurance company.

Whenever a new level of stability arose, and Keith's doctor appointments became spread out a little bit more, I let go a sigh of relief that I hadn't realized I was holding. In time, he was able to let go of some maintenance appointments because either he had improved (he began to be able to eat a wider range of food, and started to have multiple "good days" a week), or there was simply nothing else to be done (the biggest treatment advice for stress-induced IBS is to calm down and wait it out). By the end of 2016, Keith was at a place where he could let his Oregon-based medical staff go, and we were able to truly start living in Washington full time. It was exactly the break I needed so that I could fall apart.

I mean, marriage is supposed to be an equal partnership, right? I couldn't very well let Keith have all the fun.

I keep seeing you post updates and all I can think is that you're either a saint, or you're losing your mind. The words coming through the phone are from our insurance agent, Jeannine. She had been with us through the entirety of our rise and fall and had a unique view into our triumphs and struggles. From purchasing our home to celebrating the payoff of two auto loans, from building hunting for a storefront for Gearheadz to researching each expansion, Jeannine was in the background helping us to navigate (and insure) our lives. Over the years, she became much more than an insurance agent. She was one of our cheerleaders, rooting for us each step of the way.

Just before our world started to crumble, Jeannine was helping us wade through understanding insuring raw land and the construction of a log cabin. We were discussing whether to keep the house we had as a rental (our original plan) or try to sell it to cover our construction costs. She lent a great perspective to us on trying to balance our work lives and our private lives, as she was an entrepreneur herself and knew the stress that even the best of times can bring.

The conversation we were having now that we were closing on the sale of our home, after having to give up on the log cabin in the woods that we'd been working toward, was very personal. To this day, I remember sitting in my vintage Suburban, talking to Jeannine while waiting for Keith to finish an appointment. Over the preceding months, she'd cancelled or reduced all our policies as life changed, but she still cared more about me and how I was coping with our situation than she cared about the homeowner policy that I was calling to cancel.

I'm grateful that we happened upon Jeannine all those years ago, and I still try to keep in touch with how she is doing even though we're no longer negotiating policy adjustments together. I'm thankful that she continues to care about our family and am glad to consider her as one of our great friends in life and business.

VERMICULTURALIST

The farther away from normal life we progressed, the more family and friends mentioned that they were worried about me. *You can't keep going like this. You need to do something for yourself. It's not all up to you.*

Despite my outward attempt at remaining calm I was worried about me, too. I'd been entrenched in the mental health care process long enough to know that I had to take care of myself if I was going to be able to keep taking care of anyone else. I looked out into the world and tried to figure out how I could take some more time for me, that didn't involve losing more sleep.

I was already eating healthy. I do tend to eat my feelings, so my problem with food had been more of a problem of quantity than one of quality. I started going to the gym with Alison, so I had the physical side of my health covered as best I could. But I needed to get into something that could truly be mine. Something that I could do in fits and starts as I felt up to it. Something that I perceived to be of interest to no one else so that I could get some time alone.

Over the course of my lifetime, I've had ebbs and flows of hippy agricultural desires. I make most of our food from scratch, enjoy farmer's markets, make my own laundry detergent to avoid perfumes and dyes, so on and so forth. One facet of my interest in communing with nature is the idea of living off-grid and the many challenges that people face when they don't have the convenience of a plug-and-play lifestyle.

From the off-grid reading I've done, the ways people dealt with waste management has always been of particular interest. Now, I'm not just talking about composting toilets and humanure – although I'm enamored with the practice of composting toilet waste to build forest health. When I think about waste management it goes way beyond trying to convince a man with IBS to poop in a bucket, though. A family who lives off-grid has to figure out what to do with all their waste. From yard clippings to junk mail. There is a lot of information out there on self-sufficient waste management and to me, it's all interesting.

What I settled on, in our suburban home where neighbors are close, was vermiculture. If you don't have Google at the ready, vermiculture is the farming of composting worms. Essentially, they eat up all your biodegradable trash, and you use their castings (worm poop) to fertilize the garden. It's a win-win setup for everyone as it reduces the trash output from the home, while converting that refuse into usable food for plants. So, with a pile of shredded paper and some composting worms purchased from a commercial-scale worm farm, my wiggly empire began.

Vermiculture has held both literal and figurative value to me since the day we built the worm farm box. Taking the discards from our home and turning them into something useful is exactly what I knew I needed to do with my life overall. Worms are also quiet. They aren't demanding. You can feed them once a week if you work things out right. They take minimal care, and all they need from you is a place to live and shit. Every day they're out there in the box making natural fertilizer that I can use to start a garden, to grow food to feed my family. It's a way for me to feel useful, and if the worm populations increase enough, selling worms and their excess castings can be a very profitable business.

There's nothing to do with worms but observe and wait. It's a project of patience, kindness, and quiet anticipation. Baby worms may not be cute, but they're a promise of another generation of trash compactors. Another season of growth in the garden, and another chance to live closer to nature.

I owe a lot to that box of worms. In the end, they haven't saved my sanity. But they have shown me that even if all you do is eat and shit, you still can mean something to somebody. A lesson in love and care that I didn't know I needed.

I went into the worm hobby with the idea that it was something so obscure that no one would ever find any interest in it. Overall, that is true aside from the brief curiosity of people who wonder what happened to my sanity that primed me to think up such a project to begin with. But amazingly, a couple of my friends happen to be as weird as I am and find vermiculture to be as interesting as I do.

Corie and Bob have become my hippy salvation since the move from Portland (where hippies run rampant) to a small blue collar factory town that is home to two Walmarts. Corie and I found our initial bond discussing tiny house plans and micro farming setups. She took me to a class about composting, and I showed her my chicken print galoshes because I knew she'd think they were neat. We talk about gluten-free baking, artichoke growing, and share plans for gardens and bacon-wrapped simple living.

I didn't know it initially but Bob, Corie's betrothed, has been considering starting a vermicompost setup for a couple of years. He's been to the farm that I went to when I bought my worms, and we've talked about the complexities (and simplicity) of scaling up a backyard worm bin to produce compost at a commercial level.

Just this week we were at a birthday party and Bob and I started chatting about worms. My father-in-law mentioned that the family was ready to head home. *Wait a few minutes. I need to talk to Bob about worms, burlap, and hay bales.* I'm looking forward to helping Bob get his massive worm operation running, and hope that one day I'll have enough property to be his competitor.

We're going to build an empire – constructed of free-range chicken, bacon procured from happy pigs, and worm poop.

IMPATIENT PATIENT

It's January 2017. I'm writing now from a very comfortable bed at the Marriott AirPort Hotel in SeaTac, Washington, the night before a convention. I'm here to make connections, spend time with some friends, and hopefully sell a few books.

I'm also resting as much as possible. I have a bruise the size of a golf ball on my left arm, and small marks over the veins of my right. All because this week my heart decided it'd had enough. Apparently, all the years of stress that you are absorbing in the reading of this book have caught up with me. I've had a simple, asymptomatic heart murmur that was discovered when I attempted to join the Navy following my divorce in 2005. Well. It *was* asymptomatic until this week when my heart started fluttering continuously in my chest Monday morning.

I didn't want to go to the doctor, of course. I had too much to do. I felt like I was making a big deal out of nothing. But then my energy declined, a tightness took hold of my chest, and I had a splitting headache. I finally called an advice nurse, who referred me to my previous doctor's advice nurse (I still hadn't chosen a new doctor since our move), who told me to get my butt to a doctor's office, urgent care, or the emergency room as soon as possible.

The good news is, I'm not dying yet. The doctor who took care of me was very kind and gentle. She put in orders for a couple of EKGs, a host of lab work, and is sending me out to have my heart scanned to check for abnormalities. A minor problem, a simple murmur in my heartbeat, may have become a much bigger problem. We'll just have to wait and see what the tests reveal.

It's hard to swallow the truth, when the truth is that I've allowed myself to inch toward this health scare. I've believed that it was my job to make sure everything kept moving forward. I was the one who talked Keith out of closing our business when his mother died (I didn't want him to make a decision in grief that he'd later regret). I was the one that set our long hours in the shop. I was the one pushing all the home improvement projects, and lamenting the ones we couldn't complete before we came to the decision to sell our house. I worried that the closing wouldn't come through (it was delayed four times). I'm the one concerned about living off food stamps and our fall from middle-class to poverty. I've been the one stressing out over time, money, and the continual dispersal of both.

And so, here I sit. Keith is dutifully reading the manuscript for the next great novel, and making edits. I'm nursing a short glass of wine after having taken two naps and a long soak in a bathtub today – not because I'm really enjoying the vacation before the convention, but because I'm scared to death that the next heart flutter is going to be a freight train running through my chest.

One thing has been made clear to me this week, though. Despite my long history of a thousand hats, a thousand responsibilities, being the fair mom and the kick-ass wife… I can't do it all. It pains me to admit it. But I'd rather admit that I can't control life than have a heart attack, and right now those are pretty much my options.

I don't have all the answers, that much is clear. Maybe I'll have it all figured out by the time we reach the end of this book. One can only hope. Until then, an early bedtime is in my future.

I'm not going to worry about not selling enough books to cover the cost of this fluffy bed. I'm not going to worry about not selling enough books to cover the cost of the delicious burger and fries we enjoyed at dinner. I'm not going to worry about selling enough books to cover the gas, or the vendor's table, or the toiletries we had to buy in the gift shop.

Oh, who are we kidding. It's a lot to let go of. But I'm going to do my best. And hell, if you're reading this now, you're already doing your part to ease the pain.

I'm terrible at being sick. Every time I get the flu, I reach out to all the friends I've lost contact with since the last time I had the virus. I update all my blogs, tweak my website, write newsletters, and sift through hundreds of long neglected emails. If you haven't heard from me in months, and suddenly you're getting notifications by Facebook, email, blog RSS feed, and text, chances are that I've contracted a bug and I'm stuck in bed with my laptop.

One of my deepest flaws is that I feel like I have to be productive, no matter what. Maybe that productivity manifests as doing eight loads of laundry in an afternoon, or baking a pile of bread and rolls for the family. Sometimes, it turns into days of canning pineapples that were on sale for less than a dollar per fruit. You just never know with me, other than being sure that no matter where I am or what state I'm in, I'm working on something.

Part of the phenomenon is hereditary business. I come from a lengthy line of hard working women, and they not only preach that idle hands make the devil's work, but they keep that belief in active practice. I roll my eyes from time to time when I hear that my seventy-six-year-old grandmother isn't getting her flower beds moved as quickly as she'd like, and I'd sigh deep when my ninety-year-old great-grandmother would have a list of household projects for us to work on whenever I visited. I joke that I hope someday I'm able to retire and have fewer projects to do, but the reality is that I'm not quite sure how to function without work. It's an addiction, and all addictions are bad when they get out of control.

The last time I had the flu, just a couple of weeks ago, an author friend of mine named Sarah emailed to tell me that she was sorry to hear I was sick but that she was pleased to hear that I was making so much progress with my writing. That's the problem with sick days. Even if I'm too tired to chase my son around the house, too wracked by fever to make dinner or check the worm farm, I can usually pull myself together to write a couple thousand words over the course of an afternoon.

From a writing standpoint, it makes me wish all days were sick days. Although, even then, I don't feel truly productive until the day comes that I print 400 pages of manuscript out. It's a miswiring of my brain, I think, reinforced by generations of worker-bees that have come before me. As I move farther from my twenties and closer to my forties, I sense the need to slow down. Let the weeds grow, worry about stained knees and messy faces a bit less.

25¢

CRAZY PERSON

Now it's late January 2017. Over the course of writing this memoir, I have become nearly more depressed than I've been before. I haven't yet matched the worst depression I've ever experienced, thankfully. That depressive episode remains reserved for the time immediately before, during, and after my divorce from my first husband. That depression left me contemplating suicide. Let's hope I can find a way to never return to that level of despair ever again.

This present bout of depression is paired with a robust helping of anxiety. The coupling has brought me to the point of seeking medical help, both in the form of Citalopram (a generic version of the drug Celexa), and counseling. So far, the side effects from my cry for help have been both discouraging and overwhelmingly disheartening.

Here's what happened.

It has been noted by those who know me that I am pretty stressed out most of the time. I take on burdens and responsibilities that may, or may not, be mine to take on and then I equate my ability to manage those responsibilities flawlessly with self-worth. I also have a knack for compartmentalizing decades of issues of which, you can see if you've read this far, there are many. Here's a newsflash: No one can be perfect all the time, and not dealing with past heartaches and disappointments eventually catches up with the ability to slap a smile on your face and keep moving forward. Knowing that I can't be perfect and can't outwork my misery, but trying anyway, is exactly what's driven me over the edge.

This memoir has had a hand in the depression, I think, as it has made me reflect on a lot of things that I've long ignored. I mentioned that I was having crazy heart palpitations earlier, and I finally got the support I needed to wade through the poverty stricken free healthcare system to get it checked out. I saw a doctor and after crying through much of the appointment, she prescribed me the Citalopram and told me I'd feel better in a week or two. What she failed to mention was that the first week, while the drug was getting implemented into my system, was going to be hell. It's a frequent problem with drugs that tinker with your mental processes, and one that people don't generally talk about. The chemical reaction with your currently overtaxed brain isn't always rainbows and unicorns. For me, it was ten days of little sleep, no appetite, increased anxiety, and inability to sort my thoughts. I couldn't write, read, or even pay attention to my cell phone (to which I was previously permanently attached) for more than a week. Today, on day twelve of the drug, I'm finally feeling sorted out enough to type some of my thoughts.

I also started seeing a counselor in this break from my work. My first homework assignment in therapy was to start a journal in which I would write about five key points daily.

1. What emotion I'm feeling.
2. What happened today.
3. Recall a memory (happy or sad).
4. One thing I'm grateful for.
5. One thing I'm angry about.

When given the assignment, my entrepreneurial spirit kicked in, as it's always ready to do.

Me: *Can I do this as a blog?*

Counselor: (After a brief pause.) *No. A journal should be kept* private.

Me: *I'm writing a memoir. Can't I just wrap this up in that?*

Counselor: (Blank stare.) *No. It needs to be something you'll never show to anyone.*

Me: *So, I can't monetize this? People like reading about other people's* misery.

Counselor: (Deep sigh.) *What?*

Me: *I'm a writer who is trying to pay her bills. This seems like the kind of thing people would pay to read.*

I'm sure the counselor was ready to throw her hands up at this point, although she was far too professional to roll her eyes and flail in exasperation at me. I really wasn't trying to be difficult. Well, not trying too hard, anyway. As a writer who is struggling already to put words to paper, and who is making the irrational effort to be paid for it, a journaling assignment feels a bit like wasted words. Not that my feelings don't need to be expressed in a manner that is easy for me to access (writing is far easier for me to do than discussing my feelings verbally), but I doubt when faced with a CPA who is feeling down about life that she tells them to go home and do some free tax consulting for an hour each night.

But maybe she does. And I'm on the wrong side of the couch to judge.

Journaling, medication side effects, and exasperated counselors notwithstanding, I feel that I am taking the first steps on what is going to be a very long journey. I'm not even sure at this point which direction my travels are taking me, which is terrifying. After a lifetime of aiding my bipolar, schizoaffective, dual diagnosis mother, I am sure that I don't want to continue down the path of mental disorder if I can help it. And as I type from my queen size bed that's sitting on the floor of a rented room, continuing to be poverty stricken isn't feeling quite right for size, either. But beyond those two absolutes there is an entire universe of possibility and I have no idea what's going to happen next.

My hope is that I'll continue to tell stories, and that readers will stumble upon me in the years to come. My fear is that the well of writing will dry up, or that the words come out so garbled that I'll continue to flounder as an author. A related fear is that my words will be brilliant, but no one will read them until I'm dead and gone – a situation that seems to happen with some frequency, and that doesn't benefit the author deserving of praise.

Regardless of what happens, I'll keep taking these pills and writing in my private journal until instructed to do otherwise. Maybe going through the motions will be enough for a while. And after that, there'll be nowhere to go but up.

It's early 2017 and I've been challenged to do something more difficult than I've ever done before. Despite the thousand hats I've worn in my past, none of them have prepared me for this great undertaking and I'm not sure how I'm supposed to go about it. My brain buzzes when I think of it, words and feelings tumbling against the inside of my head until I have to press my thumbs against my temples and close my eyes to will them to stop. This task – this impossible task – might just be my undoing.

I have been implored to learn how to do... nothing.

The way this assignment came about was that my counselor asked me what I like to do for fun.

Me: *I like to read. Actually, I read quite a bit.*

Counselor: *What are you reading right now?*

Me: *As an author, I get a lot of requests to read other authors' works. Sometimes, the books are great. Sometimes, they aren't so great. This current one is a struggle to get through.*

Counselor: *So, you read for work. Do you read just for yourself?*

Me: *Sometimes, when I don't have a stack of other authors to read, or research to do for my next book.*

Counselor: *Okay, so you enjoy reading but you're only reading for work. That's not a hobby. What else do you like to do?*

Me: *I like to write, obviously.*

Counselor: *Right. But that's work. It doesn't count.*

Me: *I like to bake. I bake bread all the time.*

Counselor: *Oh? Tell me about that.*

Me: *Well, I started baking because Keith can't have all those preservatives. And then I started baking with whole grains because the white bread disagrees with one of the medications. And we have other friends with diet restrictions so usually I bake two or three different loaves at one time. One white, one multigrain, and sometimes one that's gluten-free, or nut-free, or lactose-free, or egg-free...*

Counselor: *That doesn't sound relaxing.*

Me: *Sure, it is. I mean, it's fun and stuff.*

Counselor: *How do you track all those different loaves while you're making them?*

Me: *Well, I set a round of timers for each loaf, and then I have to label the timers to keep track of which one is going off, and I make sure to finish the next step on one loaf before the timer goes off for another loaf...*

Counselor: *You're describing more work, you know.*

Me: ...

When I sit down and really think about it, work is what I love. Everywhere I look, I see a new project. A new business start-up. Something new to create. A way to serve others. But this conversation stuck with me for weeks, and so I agreed to attempt to spend time doing nothing. Or at least – nothing for someone else.

The endeavor has been difficult, to say the least. I've been indoctrinated into the church of Do for Others, and it's a cult that doesn't let go of its members easily. The first step I took was to stop saying yes to other people's projects. Instead, when someone comes to me asking me to do something for them, I offer to teach them to do it for themselves. Initially, it still takes time to show them how to fix whatever needs fixing, but it eliminates duplicate projects. So, although teaching someone how to sew or bake for a half hour is still a project that benefits someone else, it benefits me more. That was step one.

Next, I decided to stop feeling so guilty when I need to do something for myself. I endeavor to not feel bad if I need a nap. I attempt to not apologize to others when I need time to decompress alone. I try to do something that I want to do, without feeling bad about it, every day. Sometimes that's wandering through my mini-farm and just looking at the plants and soil (without weeding and watering). Other times it's sneaking a one-off cigarette when I'm feeling angry or overwhelmed. Or making cookies because I want a cookie, not because I want to make them to please someone else.

My last step in doing nothing for others was to start making myself a quilt. I've made dozens of quilts in my lifetime, but not even one of them has been for me. I pulled out my sewing machine, bought a bunch of fabric, and have been painstakingly assembling my own quilt that is exactly the way I want it to be. I did apologize to my husband for deciding to make a quilt that will go on our bed without any input from him, because old habits die hard and I needed his reassurance that doing this thing with only myself in mind was okay. He reminded me that I've already made him a quilt, crocheted him a blanket, recovered a couch for him, and knitted him socks.

What has happened over the last few months of trying to be more self-centered, is that I've found a release from multi-tasking. I can finally breathe deep and relax for a minute without having three projects going in tandem. I can focus on one thing at a time and although I still worry that I'm not being productive enough, I have the time to celebrate the completion of a task at the end of it.

It's going to take me a long time to finish unwinding myself from this busy bee mentality. But, for so long I've wanted a slower life, one interrupted with fewer moments of stress. I thought we'd need to move again, out of the city and away from all the people asking me to do *one more thing*… all I really had to do was start saying no and focus on myself.

Growing up, I was taught that selflessness was a requirement for salvation. But I've learned that a little bit of selfishness is needed to keep one's sanity.

MICRO-FARMER

One of the things that has spawned from my nature leaning lifestyle is the desire to be a farmer. Several years ago, when Keith and I were looking for land, the properties we attempted to purchase had to meet three requirements. First, they needed to have an area where our log cabin could be built and a place for a tiny house to sit so we could live on the property during construction. Second, the property needed to have an area that was easily accessed by a paved road so that we could install and run a paintball field as a part of Gearheadz Paintball. Third, I needed several acres to convert into a permaculture farm.

The funny thing about my dreams of farming is that I kill way more plants than I keep. I can see the irony in this, but I can't shake the desire to keep trying. I had a little garden in the shady back yard of our old house, which never really grew much beyond blackberries, potatoes, and honeysuckle because our tenth of an acre was in a planned neighborhood where the houses were crowded and sunlight was scarce.

When we moved to live with my father-in-law last year, I proclaimed that I was going to change the landscaping to have a giant garden. My late mother-in-law, Deb, was as much a keeper of plants as she was of anything else. Right now, in late February of 2017, there are thousands of bulbs springing up throughout the property. They're everywhere; in pots, in the lawn, tearing their way through the neatly graveled beds in the front yard landscaping. Years after her passing I'm busy trying not to kill off the starts I have planted in a mini-greenhouse kit in the kitchen and Deb is still pushing her green thumb into the soil outside and making the wood hyacinth proliferate.

I am getting better at the plant thing, though. I owe it to Deb's ghost undoing all the wrong I've done to these poor little plants. So far, almost all of them sprouted, and weeks after their rise from the soil almost two thirds of them are still clinging to life. Compared to my attempt at starting marigolds and lavender a few years ago, where only half of them sprouted and none of them survived long enough to be considered flowers, things appear to be trending up.

The dream has been, and as of this writing still is, to find a set of crops that can survive my care reliably enough to grow and harvest repeatedly. I decided last summer that I wasn't going to wait for the farm of "someday in the future" to figure it out though and instead started the worm farm, and tore up a huge section of lawn and lilac trees to claim as my own.

My first quasi-successful crop was a planting of buckwheat seed late in the summer. I planted the whole bed, an area about six feet deep and fifty feet long, in buckwheat. My timing was horrible. I waited until a couple of days past the last recommended planting time, and then we were hit with a blistering heatwave. Two weeks of hundred-degree weather isn't common in southwest Washington. The buckwheat waited out the heat, and amazingly much of it sprouted up as soon as the weather calmed.

The plants survived me long enough to flower, attract a plethora of pollinating insects and hummingbirds, and then went to seed. For the first time ever, I was able to cut the buckwheat stalks and set them up to dry in an attempt to harvest the seeds for later planting, or grinding up for buckwheat flour.

The drying stalks were quickly forgotten in the garage attic. The excitement of seed harvesting was replaced with the debilitating depression and anxiety of the last few pages, two science fiction convention appearances, and the editing of *Biocide*. I had a lot to clear my mind from before the tug to check out the buckwheat that had been drying for three months pulled me up to the attic again.

When I did finally pull the buckwheat out, feeling hopeful for the first time after weeks of medication and counseling, the smell of dried stalks brought a smile to my face. Buckwheat isn't a grain so it has a different smell than hay, but the sweetness of the dried stalks reminded me so much of hanging out in the barn with Oscar a lifetime ago. I set to work, thrashing seeds and separating them from the chaff.

The yield wasn't fantastic, but there's a half pint jar filled to the brim of seed that I grew on my own, harvested with the help of my four-year-old, and cleaned and packed all by myself. It's no cash crop, but it proves that with perseverance (and enough of Deb's help from beyond), this whole dream of writing novels from the patio of a farm might one day be possible.

When I was growing up, my mom kept a large garden that was split between two corners of our massive back yard. One corner held a pond, and a variety of strawberries, cucumbers, and pumpkins where we could lie and watch frogs hide under the giant vines while having a sweet snack. The other corner was a huge vegetable patch. During the seasons when Mom's faculties were intact, the vegetable patch was filled with neat rows of corn and tomatoes. But during the times when she couldn't face the world, the vegetable patch became a forest of climbing weeds, sticky thorns, and dried brush.

My own attempts at gardening have followed much of Mom's fight with nature to keep neat rows in line as sanity and time allow. For years, I'd make attempts at growing whatever seemed interesting at the time. /I'd soon abandon the rotted seeds and withered stems with a proclamation that I couldn't grow anything. It's only been recently that I've begun to see the value of learning about what grows naturally in a given area, and learning to live within nature's confines instead of trying to demand that it produce the fruits that I deem worthwhile.

The concept of paying closer attention to my failures came about when my husband and son got me a variety of seeds for Christmas. (Despite my repeated failures in the garden, they remain encouraging with my dream of farming.) One of the packets they chose for me were artichoke seeds. Although artichokes aren't widely grown in Washington, I was interested and decided to do some research on them to give them their best chance of living with me.

For years, at our old house, there was a patch of dry rocky ground just outside our front windows where thistles grew with abandon. I'd tried relentlessly to remove those damn thistles from our yard, using everything from sprays to boiling water. I pulled them by hand, carefully digging out their root systems and made sure any torn leaves went into a plastic bin so they wouldn't seed the lawn. As hard as I tried, thistles were the one plant that refused to die with my attention.

Well, as it turns out, artichokes are giant thistles. It suddenly dawned on me that maybe I needed to start learning how to cultivate this stubborn plant family that I'd had so much prolific success growing on accident. I planted those seeds, and soon I had dozens of beautiful baby thistles coming up in pots. I was excited, and carefully acclimated the four-inch-tall plants to the outdoors over the course of a couple of weeks. My son helped me to plant them, carefully carrying them to their new holes in the ground while he chatted with them about how much they'd enjoy living outside. In a hard-earned moment of clarity, I discovered the joy that gardening could bring. I felt in that moment that I'd found the key to starting the small farming venture I'd always wanted. We mulched around the plants carefully, made sure they had everything they needed for their big life outdoors, and waited for their next big growth spurt.

The cats ate them.

WOMAN WITH
TWO DOZEN HATS

Spring is nearly here. There is growth on the blueberry bushes I planted last fall, which means I've found another kind of plant that I maybe won't kill. The days are getting longer, and the sun is warmer than it's been in months. The antidepressant and counseling appear to be working. I woke up cheerful for the first time in weeks. The feeling of morning bliss didn't last forever, but it existed and was bright enough for me to recognize the feeling and make note of it.

We're still broke, still figuring out what kind of work Keith can one day return to, still not sure what we'll do if the money runs out before then. Book sales are down, but that's been the normal trend since life has interrupted my drive to promote myself and my work. A person can only do so much, and at long last I've realized that the statement is true for me as well.

The biggest realization of this time of reflection; the several months I spent writing this memoir, the past few weeks of following a counselor's guidance and trying my damndest to deal with the emotions in front of me, is that while none of my life has ever been normal, my eventual collapse certainly was. I've been working on letting go. It's a hard thing for me to do. I've been a multi-tasking, emotion diverting, project wielding super woman for too long to give it all up overnight. But the process is happening, and I hate to admit it but doing less kind of feels nice.

I can't give it all up, of course. I don't know how to function without the flux of various states of progress happening in tandem. But the whole of my accomplishments has been reduced. I'm focusing on one project at a time. I'm not doing laundry, baking bread, and doing homeschool projects with my son all at the same time. I'm not trying to run twenty errands in the span of an hour, or cramming a month's worth of correspondence into twenty minutes. I'm doing my best to focus, to take time, and to do things that benefit me before I do things that benefit others.

It's been an adjustment for everyone. I've taken care of everything for so long that it has been frustrating for those who have been used to my one-woman-solves-all method of getting things done. I've started asking for help, even with unimportant things, to relieve the pressure from myself and to prove that if I'm taking time to heal the world can keep turning without me.

So much of my drive has stemmed from feeling like I have to earn the love and respect of others by outperforming anyone's expectations, and then having to step it up the next time around because the expectations have shifted. It's a problem that I've caused for myself, and I know that it's one that I have to solve to save my health and my sanity.

The good news is, my heart is fine. My mental state is mostly intact, although it's clear to everyone that it's going to take a while for the despair of depression and the grip of anxiety to clear. There's just too much to deal with for anyone, even me, to take in stride. It's taken weeks of introspection, meditation, and forced quiet time alone to get where I'm at today. It's going to take a much longer time to reprogram myself to put less effort into things… a concept so foreign to me that just typing it makes me take pause.

I'm hanging up most of my hats. It's the only way to move forward. I'll keep the ones I love the most. Mother, partner, agriculturist, baker, and housekeeper will continue to reign supreme. And author, of course, because where would I be without the words? Despite my varied past, stories have been built in the wake of my chaos, and I can't help but write them down in the middle of the night when there simply isn't anything else to do.

Somehow, even though writing a novel-length manuscript is a monumental task that many writers spend their lives never completing, I've managed to write another book during one of the most chaotic episodes in my life. You're holding it now, and I hope you are marveling at that fact in the same way I am. Here we are at the end together. Connected through words and wondering what will come next.

ABOUT THE AUTHOR

Denise Kawaii lives and works in Longview, Washington with her husband, son, father-in-law, three cats and a bulldog. As you've read already, she keeps pretty damn busy. She writes in several genres including YA science fiction (The Adaline series), psychological crime fiction (S is for Serial as author D.K. Greene) and has dabbled in erotica (Corsets and Rum as author D.K. Wilde). All of her various personalities hang out together at KawaiiTimes.com.

ABOUT THE ARTIST

Maggie Love is a Los Angeles based artist and illustrator, though she hails from the tiniest of towns in central Maine. She draws and paints retro inspired devilish dames and other things that go bump in the night. You can find her on Instagram at: @StarkGravingMad, or at StarkGravingMad.com